EVERYONE
CAN WRITE

A guide to get you started

HOWARD GELMAN

EXISLE
PUBLISHING

First published 2014

Exisle Publishing Pty Ltd
'Moonrising', Narone Creek Road, Wollombi, NSW 2325, Australia
P.O. Box 60–490, Titirangi, Auckland 0642, New Zealand
www.exislepublishing.com

A CiP record for this book is available from the National Library of Australia

ISBN 978 1 921966 51 4

Design and typesetting by Christabella Designs
Typeset in Minion 10/18pt
Printed in Shenzhen, China, by Ink Asia

This book uses paper sourced under ISO 14001 guidelines from well-managed forests and other controlled sources.

10 9 8 7 6 5 4 3 2 1

Disclaimer

While this book is intended as a general information resource and all care has been taken in compiling the contents, this book does not take account of individual circumstances and is not a substitute for professional advice. Neither the author nor the publisher and their distributors can be held responsible for any loss, claim or action that may arise from reliance on the information contained in this book.

CONTENTS

HOW TO USE THIS BOOK

So you want to write something. You feel an urge to tell a story, perhaps about your ancestors and how they came here. Maybe it's a story about the company you started and the legacy you want to leave your children. Of course, some of us are forced to become writers. You may have been drafted to write the newsletter for your volunteer organisation, which will be crucial in the next donation drive. Or perhaps your boss wants a tightly written, complete factual account of the company's activities that will be the next quarterly report. Get out your writing tools and start.

Or you might want to jump into the world of the Internet. You have a lot to say about some pretty important ideas in your daily work. You'd like to open a blog and see if your ideas match or provoke others in your field. You start to think of those essays compiled in English classes. Do you remember how to do it? It wasn't easy and you vowed to put all that school stuff behind you. But now it seems it might come in handy. How do you write an essay anyway?

There are a lot of reasons for us to look at our writing skills critically and decide to improve and upgrade our ability to communicate through writing. *Everyone Can Write* gives you the tools to achieve your writing goals. However, I don't expect anyone to read it from beginning to end, although that wouldn't be a bad idea. If you jump to sections that answer your questions, that's a good way to get useful information and you can re-read any section for a refresher.

Part 1, 'The Basics', gives you the basic yet essential techniques and rules to get started with your writing. Chapter 1, 'Technique', is simple. I show you how to be your own editor and to make decisions about your writing. To do this, I've organised a three-step process, called pre-write, free write, rewrite. Understanding how to apply this formula will cut through most of the difficulty we face in writing. I also explain how to distinguish between being a writer and being an editor, which is a key to understanding the writing process.

Chapter 2, 'Grammar', explains the rules simply and clearly so you can immediately apply them to your writing. These instructions are the main elements in the editing task. All of these items are meant to promote your rewriting skills. What, you don't want to know grammar? You only want to know how to write. I understand any reticence about a book that promotes learning grammar, however the two are connected. In Part 1 I give you practical information that will definitely help you to write more clearly. This includes tips I've put together in my years of being an editor, writer, teacher and writing coach. These instructions will work if you apply them. Do it and tell me what happens.

Part 2, 'Types of Writing', forms the core of the book. Chapters 3, 4 and 5 explain how to impart facts in a report; how to tell a story in a narrative; and how to develop an argument in an essay. In these chapters I discuss the basic structure of each approach to writing.

The report is the tool of commerce and business, and presents a factual approach to information communication. Knowing the difference between the report and the essay is essential to achieving your communication goals. What usually happens in business is choosing the wrong structure for disseminating information. We end up with long-winded documents that overload us with facts and figures, when we are looking for a quick and clear answer to a request.

The narrative stands alone. It is storytelling and sometimes we mistake the fictional use of narrative for the non-fiction one. In this book we are not discussing fiction, poetry, playwriting or screenwriting. In non-fiction narratives — biography, autobiography or memoir — we have to tell real stories with actual people, places and situations. It can be just as dramatic and intense as the more creative approach of fiction, but the rules are different. In fact, telling a true story may be the most elemental writing task. It even pops up in essays and reports.

Many of us dealt with the essay either in high school or tertiary education. We may even have some misgivings about taking up this task again. But it is the standard method for explaining an argument and the structure is familiar to most of you. If you read magazines or newspaper columnists or the latest bloggers, you will be familiar with the essay format. For the budding e-writer who wants to carve out an Internet spot, learning how to hone a well-written essay is the key to communication success. Fortunately, there is a simple method to conquer this dreaded exercise of our schooldays.

Start with any one of these approaches to writing — report, narrative or essay. The key is to know whom you are writing for and what your goals are. When you write that family history for all your relatives, you will have to tell them where and when the story began. If you are getting information to your business clients you will need to understand the business box of report writing. If you are demonstrating how to think through hypotheses, write an essay. Choose your format and then you can apply the rules outlined in Part 1. Follow the rules and you will succeed in writing clear, easy-to-read and interesting documents.

Chapter 6, 'Email writing', deals with communicating succinctly and successfully in an email. I show how my writing method, using bullet points and appropriate spacing, can help you become a better communicator in what can often be an ill-considered form of communication.

A word about style. I believe style is something writers have to want to develop. That is, you have to be aware of how you write and how sentence structure and word placement can affect your writing. I call this the architecture of writing and I have several examples about how to build a piece of writing and maintain clarity.

The book ends with the 'Guide to usage' chapter, an alphabetical listing of specific items with explanations. These are ones I think most often challenge the everyday writer. This could be the difference between 'its and it's' or when to use 'among' or 'between'.

Everyone Can Write is deliberately short and concise. I want it to be portable, something you can carry in a briefcase or keep in a drawer at work. I wouldn't mind if you carried it in your back pocket and opened it only when you need confirmation that a split infinitive is okay in the sentence you just wrote. I also want the book to be an easy read and offer unambiguous explanations. That's as complicated as I hope this will get, except I'd like you to use it often and discover for yourself what works and what doesn't. So stop looking at a blank screen and start writing.

PART 1
The Basics

1

TECHNIQUE

You need it

Many novice and experienced writers struggle with the problem of starting that very first sentence. They stare at a blank screen for hours or pace the floor and do anything but start writing. This chapter will not only get you writing that starter sentence, it will give you techniques to better organise your time and continue writing. It will also help you to be your own editor, so you'll know when to rewrite that opening sentence. Overall, this will improve your writing and you'll have an effective method to fall back on. This takes some effort. However, I believe that practice and reading good models are excellent ways to improve on technique.

Let's start with that tricky first sentence. We'll then take a look at ten rules you can use that will improve your skill level and result in clear, easy-to-follow writing. Next we'll explore a way to better use your time with my formula: pre-write, free write, rewrite.

The first sentence

A problem that technique can solve is the first-sentence syndrome. Many people find it difficult to write that first sentence. For the beginning writer, this can be an insurmountable stumbling block. I have listened even to practising writers tell of their despair at trying to get that first sentence on the screen.

You want to say, 'It's just a sentence. Just write it.' But, it's not that simple. After hearing this lament from many students and writers, I know that the complaint is serious and it requires a solution. I call the solution 'sentence starters'.

You should compile a list of easy-to-use sentence starters for each kind of document. Let's make a list of possible sentence starters for a business report:

> *The following subjects will be discussed in this report: …*

> *This report will cover the best methods for …*

> *The major focus of this report will be …*

We can do the same thing for a narrative approach. In this style of writing you are usually writing a story, so you have some creative leeway. You might want to start with a quote or description. In each of the following sentences, you are trying to grab the reader's attention:

> *'I lost a fortune in two hours but I'll make another tomorrow,' said …*

He was five years old but had an adult's vocabulary.

With the essay, the easiest approach is to restate the premise or argument. If your essay question is 'Are millions of dollars in government bailouts an effective way to support the local car manufacturing industry?' your first sentence might be:

The government faces a dilemma trying to support the car manufacturing industry with millions of dollars in bailouts.

This reiterates the premise in a declarative sentence. It's a method that has worked for students taking exams and writing essay papers. Don't invent a new process. Rely on what has worked for writers in the past.

The way to break the opening-sentence syndrome is to have a solution before you start. The success of the solution is not writing the sentence but in starting the whole writing process. That is, by writing the first sentence, you are able to finish the paragraph, the chapter and even the book.

Best of all, you can change your opening sentence when you start rewriting (which is covered later in this chapter). In most cases you will see a better way to introduce the first paragraph of your report, narrative or essay. That's why these sentences are called 'starters'. Use them to start and then discard them. It is another editing tool that helps you to overcome an obstacle. You can even start using marginal words, such as *however, therefore* or *in addition.* All are helpful starter words, but in the final version of reports and narratives they can be deleted.

A good way to keep track of these devices is to compile an editorial toolkit, that is, a file on your desk or on your desktop. You can keep all your records in this editorial box. Samples of opening sentences that you've read in other journals or reports can be stored for future inspiration. You might want to add notes you've made on possible writing topics or quotes you think can be used in future projects.

The point here is for the writer to be in control of the writing. I want you to make a decision about each sentence, even if this takes a nanosecond. When you know why you wrote a sentence then you are in control of the words, not the other way around. I often hear students say, 'It just came out that way'. Remember, though: this is not fiction where the characters sometimes take over the author. In non-fiction prose you are in control of the words. The rule is to be clear, simple and forceful.

Writing can be hard work. It can also run off your typing fingers like melted butter. Sometimes it comes easily and sometimes not. All writers face that opening problem. All of us have a technique when we write, whether we know it or not.

The ten rules

Now that we've tackled the opening sentence, let's look at ways to keep your writing going. English works best in short declarative sentences, statements of fact, particularly for non-fiction writing as we are discussing in this book. When you are confident writing in this simple declarative style, you can then use stylistic devices such as a compound sentence or a subordinate clause to good effect (for more on these, see 'Technique' p. 11 and 'Guide to usage', p. 146).

Here are ten queries to ask about the structure of your writing:

1. How many words in a sentence?
2. How many sentences in a paragraph?
3. How do you identify the parts of a sentence?
4. How do you recognise active and passive sentences?
5. How do you use the dependent clause or modifier?
6. How do you recognise an adverb when you see one?
7. How do you know where to use a pronoun?
8. How do you use the semi-colon and colon?
9. How do you know where to put the comma?
10. How do you know when you're finished?

These rules are easy to incorporate in your writing and apply equally to report writing, non-fiction narrative, essay writing and emails. Each of the rules will be discussed in more detail in chapters 3, 4 and 5. It will be helpful for everyone to read the section in Chapter 3, 'Report writing'. Here, you will find the most detailed examples of how the ten rules work. And if you're scratching your head thinking, 'What on earth is an adverb?' then turn to Chapter 2, 'Grammar'.

You can return to these rules when you're in the 'rewriting' stage of your writing (see p. 21). If you follow the rules, you will be able to produce simple and clear writing. What they provide is a reader-friendly style. Once you feel you have mastered the simple sentence (don't confuse simple sentences with simple ideas), you can experiment with style (see p. 25).

Pre-write, free write, rewrite

Now we have to think about allocation of time. How you distribute your time is key to getting the job done and working at an efficient rate. This doesn't mean you will accomplish these tasks quickly or in less time than you now spend writing; what we are striving for is the best use of time and an increase in the readability of your work.

There are three elements that make up the task of writing: research, writing, editing. Or, as the following formula puts it: pre-write, free write, rewrite. These three activities should dictate the method you use to complete any writing task you undertake. If you follow this routine you will be able to adapt it to your time schedule and writing habits. Here's how it works.

Pre-writing covers all your preliminary research. This can mean hours on the Internet or at the local library, or looking up one source for a quote. The content of your writing will dictate how much time you need to spend on pre-writing. For reports, you will gather information, facts, figures and testimonials or maybe you will have the answer to a request in a file on your computer. The majority of your pre-write will be informational.

With a narrative, you might be looking at genealogical tables and tracking travel documents or poring over photographs. You might be trying to decipher handwritten letters from one hundred years ago. Again, the pre-writing task could even change as you start to write. You might have to retrace your steps and start at the beginning.

If you write a personal opinion piece for the letters section of the newspaper, you might not do any research at all. You know your subject after years of reflection and don't need to refer to any other sources. You are ready to write. Or your essay might require long-distance travel and immersion in the subject matter over many months before you feel confident that you understand your task and can start writing. Pre-writing is a key element in the writing process, and we have all built up habits and approaches that we use. It is a variable element and you will have to deal with it.

The next step in the process gets us into the actual task of writing — it's what I call **free writing**. But there is a crucial point here: this first writing effort is almost automatic writing. It involves getting down all the research and complicated thinking you have done on the subject. Get your facts and arguments on the computer screen (or note pad) and, if possible, don't stop until you've finished. The object here is to reach a goal. It might be completing a chapter, or only a page, but you have to write to that end point.

Sometimes you have to stop in the middle or before you have reached your end point if you run out of steam or you have to work on another task. So how do you get back into free-writing mode? The best approach is to retrace your writing back to a beginning point and start reading. At this stage, don't correct or edit or try to change what you've written. You are reading to get into the mood of free-writing, like an athlete warming up. When you come to the last sentence, start free writing again and work to the goal.

Once you reach that target, and it might be one page or ten, you'll have to stop and go back to where you started. Don't panic — you are entering a new phase as a writer. Now you are going to become the editor of your writing and **rewrite**. Turn on the tracking function in your Word document, known as 'track changes' (if you are using another word-processing software you will need to find the equivalent function). Tracking gives you the tools of editing you'll need for rewriting. It allows you to see all the changes you have made and are about to make to your document. You can turn tracking on and off. Get used to the tracking device as you change your role from writer to editor.

The more pages you include in your initial free-writing stint the easier it will be to use tracking since you won't have to turn it on and off when you switch tasks. Rewriting is the most important element in the process as it results in better writing. Now is the time to apply the ten rules outlined earlier. Work your way down the list of rules, editing sentences and paragraphs. Using the 'track changes' function, you can switch from 'final' to 'final showing mark-up' or back to 'original' so you can see how the final version will appear once you have finished making all your changes and corrections.

The crucial difference between free writing and rewriting is this change from writer to editor. When rewriting, you are practising being the editor of your own writing. In a sense, you are distancing yourself from your initial words and coming to them with a fresh perspective. It can even help to have a rest before beginning editing to clear your mind and approach the work as if you were reading it for the first time.

Here is what these three approaches look like when we allocate our time:

- Pre-write: 10–40%
- Free write: 10%
- Rewrite: 50–80%

Notice that the two variables are pre-write and rewrite. The constant is the free writing stage. Your goal is always to use free writing to get the words on the screen. Pre-writing and rewriting will vary according to the amount of research required for each project.

This is not an exact science with precise measurements. With this system as a guide, you will gauge how to allocate your time and what works best for each project. You may only be able to free write one page at a time, which means having a second rewrite when the document is finished. Or, having done the research, your free writing might take you to the end of the document without stopping. Having finished the free writing draft in one sitting, you can now be the editor and can work from start to finish applying the rules and pruning the document.

Understand the visual impact of your document

Word processing has taken over all the manuscript marking we used to do as editors. Now with tracking, cutting and pasting, we can manipulate the page endlessly and get the results we want. Oddly, not many writers outside of publishing use these tools. Yet they are easy for anyone to learn and 'full screen' mode can be effective for an overview of any manuscript.

Seeing how the words appear on the page is crucial to whether you have a reader-friendly result, and the rewriting stage is the time to think about the visual display. Using the 'full screen' or 'print preview' modes to view your work can be helpful for this. Consider the margin-to-margin full screen disclaimers on websites. These are long-winded, reader-unfriendly tracts of writing and written not to be read. They break every rule of spacing and sentence construction.

A reader's eye reacts positively to white space and relatively short sentences. If you want your writing to be read, then pay attention to paragraphing and sentence length. With reports, keep sentences to fewer than 25 words (Rule 1) and paragraphs short (three to four sentences) according to Rule 2. For narratives, provide even more white space and where possible use quotes to break up the text.

The essay allows you to expand paragraphs, but not too much.

Since you are concentrating on linking ideas, paragraphs need to have a beginning, middle and end. However, use 'full screen' or 'print preview' mode to check that each page looks accessible.

All about style

If our technique is consistent and we use it with confidence, we call that style. We develop our sense of style by experimenting with sentences and words. When you get to that level in your writing, you may want to look at how a sentence works dramatically.

We associate the word 'drama' with plays but the broader definition is when your description controls the meaning in a way that keeps your reader enthralled until the exact arrangement of the words reveals all. The structure of a dramatic sentence is easy to dissect. Here is a simple sentence with a missing element. See if you can fill in the blank:

> *Laughing quietly, he reached under the log and passed me a large …*

You can see that we can't make sense of those words. We can get some of the meaning but there's something important missing, something so important that complete sense can't be obtained without it. The finished sentence might look like this:

Laughing quietly, he reached under the log and passed
me a large green frog.

The thought content of the sentence suddenly becomes complete with the addition of two words — 'green frog'. Of course, not all sentences make sense at the very end. Some make good sense early and some make a good deal of sense somewhere in the middle. Once you understand how to arrange words deliberately so they come together in a reader's mind exactly where you want them to, you will have mastered an important aspect of narrative writing.

We can call the point at which meaning becomes clear the **sense point**. When you have a dramatic scene to describe, using the sense point to your advantage can make a difference in keeping the reader enthralled in your subject. To do this, we need to know what happens when we shift the sense point in a sentence.

Here are some sentences describing the scene of a brutal murder. Our objective is to draw the most drama out of the retelling of the events. We can construct this crucial sentence once we identify the sense point. Let's consider the result if you decide to put the sense point toward the beginning of the sentence:

> *He pulled a human head from the sack, its hair twisted in his fingers.*

The sense point, 'human head', is the first bit of information the reader sees. If you decide to put the sense point closer to the middle of the sentence, it might read like this:

> *He reached into the sack and pulled out a human head, its hair twisted in his fingers.*

Here the information simply flows and you get the meaning in one read through. However, if you want to create a sense of dread and suspense by keeping the reader waiting, you can place the sense point at the very end, like so:

> *He reached into the sack and, twisting its hair in his fingers, pulled out a human head.*

If you look closely at these three sentences, you'll probably begin to realise the control you can exert over your language once you identify the elements of the sentence. In the last sentence, the sense point seems to linger after a pause and the reader suddenly gets the whole picture. Keeping the reader guessing until the very end adds drama and suspense. It also allows you to control the story.

Some writers are able to juxtapose the sense point easily and others must work a bit harder to achieve this. We sometimes call this 'the ability to tell a joke' because jokes usually require keeping the punch line hidden until the end of the story. Some people are good at telling jokes and others give away the punch line too early. When you master how to tell a good joke, you will know how to use the sense point effectively.

Working out how to orchestrate a sentence to gain a particular reaction from your reader means you are looking deeply into developing a style in your writing. You begin to use a variety of techniques (such as the ones we have illustrated) to entice your reader. You might want an informal, conversational style that treats the reader as a confidant. Or you might want to be out of the picture and present the facts as up-front as possible. You will alter your style to suit the audience and the content. It will happen as you continue to work — style is inevitable for writers.

Proofreading

One more task remains in order to finish your project — proofreading. This may seem a simple and perfunctory exercise but it is important. Even well-written prose can be undermined by spelling and grammar errors, especially if they occur on the first page.

Using the word-processing spell check is helpful but not fully reliable. The best method is to have someone new to the project be the proofreader. Professional companies pay for experts to do this. The rest of us have to rely on friends and colleagues.

2

GRAMMAR

Easier than you think

Novice writers tend to be afraid of grammar. They might have bad memories of mistakes they made, or they never really received proper instruction in grammar. What they know is instinctive. But do you know the correct answer to these grammatical puzzles: Is it 'I' or 'me'? What is the subject of this sentence?

Which one is the passive sentence? What is a dependent clause? Do I understand how a sentence works? Questions about grammar lurk in the background as you start writing.

This chapter is not going to offer a complicated analysis of English grammar. There are many books to consult if you have an interest in a more detailed understanding of how words work together and how their position in sentences is accomplished. We won't be doing that. What you need for your writing is a simple explanation of the basic sentence so you understand your objective. A good deal of English grammar is instinctive if you are a native speaker, so you already know more than you think.

For non-native speakers there are many courses available which will assist you not only in understanding the English language but also enable you to get a better grasp of English grammar. Check the Internet for accredited courses in your local area. I recommend taking one or more of these official courses.

The tools we use to construct a sentence are the building blocks of our language. They are: nouns, pronouns, verbs, adjectives and adverbs. These are the types of words that make up the bulk of the dictionary, which gives an alphabetical list of their meanings. There are other words used as connectives and before and after phrases; most of these are part of our instinctive use of the language. However, to start with let's take a quick look at each of these types of basic word.

A **noun** is the word for a person, place or thing — for example 'woman', 'playground', 'chair' (note that the names of people and places — e.g. Joanne, Los Angeles, Australia — are called proper nouns and start with a capital letter). A **pronoun** can substitute for a noun — some examples include 'I', 'she', 'they' and 'it'. A **verb** describes action, such as 'jump', 'swam', 'sit' and 'talk'. An **adjective** modifies or tells us something about a noun — 'a *wooden* chair', '*brown* hair', 'a *cold* night'. Finally, **adverbs** modify or tell us something about a verb — 'he talked *loudly*', 'she ran *quickly*', 'they jumped *excitedly*'.

Using the building blocks to
construct a sentence

What we need to know is how these building blocks — nouns, pronouns, verbs, adjectives and adverbs — are put together to make sentences. Here is how it's done. The English sentence has a basic structure, to which there are three essential parts — subject, verb, object. Let's start with the **subject**.

Jack delivered the package.

I left my car in the garage.

The subject can be a noun or pronoun. In the first sentence 'Jack', a noun, is the subject. This is what the sentence is about: Jack. In the second sentence, 'I', a pronoun, is the subject. That is what the sentence names.

The subject is the noun that performs the action and the verb is how the subject carries out or enacts what is happening. The **verbs** in these two sentences are 'delivered' and 'left'. These describe the action that takes place. (Note that verbs are sometimes described to children as 'doing words', which can help you remember their function in a sentence).

Here's a slight variation on the first sentence:

He has delivered the package.

In this sentence, the verb is 'has delivered' and in this case it is known as a verb phrase.

Subjects and verbs can be simple or complete. The examples above use simple one-word subjects. Let's now take another example:

The angry driver refused to leave his car.

In this case the complete subject is 'the angry driver' and the complete verb phrase is 'refused to leave'. We call them 'complete' because they comprise more than one word (the subject, in this example, comprises both an adjective — angry — and a noun — driver). These two elements are linked. Find the verb in the sentence and ask yourself who or what is driving that verb — or, to put it another way, who or what is doing the action the sentence describes — and you have found the subject.

The direct **object** is the receiver of the action.

Sam hit the ball.

Here 'Sam' is the subject, 'hit' is the verb and 'the ball' is the direct object. Note that I have referred to this as the 'direct' object; there are two kinds of objects — direct and indirect. The direct object is the receiver of the verb; it's the ball that is hit. An indirect object is when the verb is giving something or taking something. It always comes before the direct object, as in:

Let me give it to Sam.

The indirect object is 'it'; 'give' is the verb, and the direct object or receiver is 'to Sam'.

So, if the subject is what the sentence is about, and the verb is the doing or action thing, then the object is the receiver of what is happening.

Passive and active sentences

Let's move on to something a little more complex:

The ball was hit by Sam.

In this version we have changed the subject and come up with a different result. We have, in effect, switched subjects, so that the subject is now 'the ball', and the outcome is called a passive sentence. That is, Sam was the doer in the first, active version and is now the passive doer in the second one.

Many discussions of grammar advise that active sentences are preferable and passive sentences should be avoided. However, the passive sentence can be useful, especially when you want to disguise the subject of the sentence or change the tone of your writing, perhaps to slow down the pace. Here's an example of this idea in action:

Mistakes were made but the project will go ahead.

This shows that passive sentences can be used to good effect when you want to give a positive result without naming the person responsible for the mistakes. The focus of your writing should be to recognise when you are writing passive or active sentences so you can choose which is the best version for the context. One clue is that an active sentence usually starts with a doer, a person as its subject. To use the above example, this might then become:

> *James and his team made many mistakes but the project will go ahead.*

Clauses and more complex sentences

A group of words that includes both a subject and verb is called a **clause**. The sentences below are both complete clauses. We call them **simple sentences**.

> *The bridge collapsed.*

> *We had no insurance.*

As you build sentences, you can use more than one subject and verb and connect these elements in complicated structures. We can build one sentence by joining two independent clauses, as in:

The bridge collapsed and we had no insurance.

They were combined by using 'and'. We often write this kind of **compound sentence** using connecting words such as: 'and', 'but', 'for', 'or', 'nor', 'so' and 'yet'. It is a simple and useful device for varying the style of our writing. By combining simple and compound sentences, we allow the pace of reading to vary, and we avoid monotony and boring the reader.

Another structure is the **complex sentence**. It contains one dependent clause and one independent clause. Let's go over what that means. A **dependent clause** is a group of words that looks like a sentence but the group needs something more in order to become complete. The dependent clause works when it is joined to an independent clause, that is, a group of words that makes a complete sentence.

Because it was poorly designed

You can tell when you read this aloud that it is not complete; something is missing. There is an easy way to locate dependent clauses. They start with what are called **marker words**, such as 'because' in this example. Others are: 'after', 'although', 'as', 'as if', 'before', 'even if', 'even though', 'if', 'in order to', 'since', 'though', 'unless', 'until', 'whatever', 'when', 'whenever', 'whether' and 'while'.

When we attach this dependent clause to an independent clause (notice that I started this sentence with 'when'), we get a complex sentence.

Because it was poorly designed, the bridge collapsed.

Now the sentence is complete. The two clauses make up a complete sentence. One point to remember is that the independent clause should always start with the implied subject of the preceding dependent clause. The subject in the dependent clause above is 'it' but the subject that gives the sentence clarity is 'the bridge'.

Here is the progression in how sentences work. First is the simple sentence.

Commercial orchards in the Hunter Valley are shrinking.

Growers must act.

These are two simple complete sentences. We can combine them into a compound sentence:

Commercial orchards in the Hunter Valley are shrinking and growers must act.

Or we can connect them by forming a dependent and independent clause to make up a new sentence.

Because commercial orchards in the Hunter Valley are shrinking, growers must act.

'Growers must act' is the independent clause that completes the sentence.

One more device to increase your sentence-writing ability is the **compound complex sentence**, where we use a connecting word and a dependent clause. Here, we combine the two methods by starting with a marker word, 'because', and a connecting word, 'and'.

Because commercial orchards in the Hunter Valley are shrinking, growers must act and they should enlist the aid of local politicians.

You will also note that this sentence, the longest of the four versions, is only 21 words. So you can write compound complex sentences and still stay under the 25-word limit for reports and essays as well. (For more on Rule 1, 'How many words in a sentence?' turn to p. 62.)

Using adjectives and adverbs

Now that we know how to vary sentences, we can discuss using words to bring out greater meaning for the reader. We have at our disposal many modifiers, or words that add a new or different meaning to our sentences. These are called adjectives and adverbs. **Adjectives** come in many shapes and kinds. An adjective can be a single word such as 'blue', as in, 'the blue book', or it can be a group of words, such as 'the *small, blue picture* book'. In each case, an adjective tells us more about the noun 'book'.

An interesting use of adjectives shows that we can employ

them in three different ways. Let's look at 'good', 'better' and 'best', the three forms of meaning starting with 'good'. Each change enhances the meaning of 'good'. You can do this to most adjectives. Sometimes the original word remains, as in 'bright', 'brighter', 'brightest', or 'angry', 'angrier', 'angriest'. What this shows is that you have a lot of words with subtle changes in meaning when you apply adjectives to modify nouns.

Adverbs serve a similar function. They modify the verb. Since verbs describe what's happening, the adverb tells us something about the time or place and the type of action. Adverbs are all around us: 'speaks *slowly*', 'wakes *early*', 'eats *voraciously*'. These are the 'ly' versions of adverbs, the largest group. There are other adverbs without this ending, such as 'sits *still*', 'runs *fast*'. However, it is the 'ly' ending that we are concerned with.

When we are writing reports with facts and information, adverbs work against clear writing. Because they undercut the verb, which drives the information, they should be avoided or at least kept to a minimum in report writing. An example will clearly show you why:

I will probably be able to deliver the report this afternoon.

I will be able to deliver the report this afternoon.

While the first sentence may be true, it conveys uncertainty, which means you should resolve it before delivering the message. In business, you solve the problem before you write the second sentence.

In essay writing, the adverb conveys the subtle changes and modification that we expect:

The second argument is probably the strongest; however, there are some criticisms about this point of view.

In this sentence, the adverb 'probably' prepares the reader for the censure in the next clause. Since the key to essay writing is linking ideas, adverbs are useful modifiers and connectors. Some adverbs, like adjectives, can denote comparative degree, as in 'fast', 'faster', 'fastest', or 'soon', 'sooner', 'soonest'. What we want to avoid is loading sentences down with too many adjectives and adverbs. Use them *precisely* and *sparingly*, as I've done in this sentence.

Punctuation

Sentences are also created with more than words. We use marks such as full stops (known as periods in US usage), commas, semi-colons and colons to create the pace of our sentences. It is as if we are trying to tell the reader when to take a breath, when to pause, when to start again and when to stop. We use the **full stop** to end every sentence, except when we ask a question (?), issue a command (!) or declare with an exclamation. A full stop is final. That's the end of the sentence. Take a split second to pause and consider the sentence and then go on.

But within the sentence the next most frequently used punctuation mark is the **comma**. It is used to change the reader's pace and give meaning to phrases and clauses within the complete sentence. The placement of commas also helps us understand the sentence in a quick reading. For example, a comma can be used to separate two independent clauses when they are joined into a compound sentence by 'and', 'but', 'for', 'or', 'so' and 'yet'.

> *I reviewed the facts, and concluded that the project*
> *was poorly designed.*

The comma comes before the connecting word and the two sentences are joined.

A comma also sets off a dependent clause before we get to the main clause:

> *After reviewing the facts, I concluded that the*
> *project was poorly designed.*

The comma separates the two clauses and completes the sentence.

Commas can also set off a clause in the middle of a sentence:

> *I concluded, after reviewing the facts, that the*
> *project was poorly designed.*

When a phrase or clause appears in the middle of a sentence, the use of a comma may be the link to understanding the meaning of the sentences. Here is an example to illustrate the classic use of a comma to convey precise meaning:

The teacher said the student was an idiot.

The teacher, said the student, was an idiot.

In the first case, the student is the idiot; in the second, the teacher is the idiot. The use of commas around the clause is the difference between two completely different meanings. Commas are also used in a list of three or more items, such as:

He bought a bag, a jacket, a tie and a rope.

This is British and Australian usage. In the US, we would add the third serial comma before 'and':

He bought a bag, a jacket, a tie, and a rope.

A comma can also be used to set off a person's title:

Jack Edwards, the CEO, concluded that the project was poorly designed.

Other uses of the comma are mainly to prevent possible confusion or misreading. It is a way of guiding the reader to the meaning you are intending.

Sometimes we confuse the use of the comma and another punctuation mark, the semi-colon. The **semi-colon** has two specific purposes and should not be overused. It can join two independent clauses into one sentence. But the guiding principle here is that the two sentences must be closely related, so close that the writer believes joining them adds to the overall meaning.

That is a tall order. Many beginning writers think semi-colons add to the complexity of the writing so they load them on. However, used without careful attention the semi-colon just adds to the confusion. In report writing, my rule is: don't use them! Avoid the semi-colon because it is usually misused and forces the reader to decipher what the writer intended. Is there any time that we can use a semi-colon? Yes, the semi-colon has a place in essay writing but only if we are careful about using it. For example, the semi-colon can join two sentences when also using an adverb:

I reviewed the facts; consequently, I have concluded
the project was poorly designed.

Using a conjunctive adverb together with a semi-colon to link these two thoughts makes the result seem final and definite. It is better than:

I reviewed the facts; I have concluded the project
was poorly designed.

Here, simply using a semi-colon doesn't add anything; in fact, it seems awkward. In essay writing the semi-colon can be an interesting stylistic device. I suggest that you should work with them sparingly until you feel you know how they can add to the meaning of the sentence.

In narrative writing a semi-colon can also be a useful device, particularly when describing people or events. Here you can think about joining short sentences to create an atmosphere and mood:

He was tall; he had a way of walking; it made him
look like a swaying flagpole.

The three clauses paint a picture of the man, and by attaching them with semi-colons into one sentence the description is strengthened. It's a useful way of painting with words.

One more punctuation mark to understand is the colon. Like the full stop it has a definite and clear usage. The **colon** indicates that something is going to be explained. Stop the sentence with a colon and then give the information. What follows could be a list of words, a set of bullet points, or a piece of information that explains why you have set it off in the sentence.

There is only one thing to do: call the council and complain.

This is the information use of the colon. But using it to introduce bullet points means adding a necessary word:

We will need the backing of the following officers:

- *President*

- *Treasurer*

- *Secretary*

- *Council members.*

We should contact them immediately.

The formal introductory word here is 'following'. If you introduce a list with this word, a colon usually comes after.

A colon also introduces a quote.

Jack Edwards, the CEO, ended the meeting saying: 'All the facts are now available. We can see that the project was poorly organised and didn't fulfil the company's requirements.'

The colon also has some specialised uses not related to sentences. It appears in reference notes, time and date lists, and salutations.

These are the punctuation marks that orchestrate your sentences. You have a toolkit at your disposal — full stop (period), comma, semi-colon, colon — and the way you employ them dictates how readable your final result will be. Use them wisely and with a smile.

What I have discussed is a brief overview of grammar for a practical outcome. You now have the basic knowledge that gives you some insight into writing. These are things you already know instinctively. Sentences are not unfamiliar. You have been writing them for years. The difference should be that this chapter has given you the impetus to take greater control of your writing. That means raising your skill level. The more you know why you are writing a sentence, the better the outcome.

PART 2

Types of Writing

3

REPORT WRITING

Get the facts

If you work in the world of business, you will be expected to turn out readable pieces of written communication. These could be board reports, executive summaries, publicity items and even correspondence such as a job résumé or application. We call this kind of writing business reporting.

The world of business and report writing relies on getting facts from one place to another.

We usually know one structure for writing documents and that is the essay. However, let's be emphatic about this: the essay structure — introduction, body, conclusion — doesn't work for business reports or emails. In fact, it works against succeeding in writing good business documents. (I'll give you a more positive view of the essay in a later chapter.)

Most of us who write learned to do so in school. We wrote essays in high school and then for university courses. Some of us actually had instruction on how to write an essay. We were given models to read and, if we were lucky and old enough, shown how English grammar works. It could be baffling or instructive. Unfortunately, what we were taught about writing in school is of little help in the world of business communication.

Today, essay writing is the work of the specialist and not really helpful in the workplace. We need something simpler and more direct. Most of us in business or private communication need to get to information quicker and make our decisions faster, and the essay is the long way around.

The business box

We all know that today's world requires a great deal of reading and analysing, and the simpler the communication the better. I sometimes ask my students to be split personalities, that is, to write one way in their Philosophy course and another way in my course. For all of us who have left school behind, the business box technique will serve us better. For writing a report we need to look at what journalists do.

The business box is a simple technique that uses the journalists' approach to writing. Their writing structure resembles the shape of an inverted pyramid, as seen on the left-hand side of the following diagram:

THE INVERTED PYRAMID

LEAD
Details

Most important

Least important

(straight
news
story)

THE BUSINESS BOX

**News lead answers the
5 W's and H query.
Business lead answers
who and what**

Transition paragraphs provide
details to support lead. This is
essential information and key to
understanding the report.

Closing paragraphs are the least
important. In a business document
you can re-state the lead at the
close of your report.

The inverted pyramid is how journalists have been writing for over one hundred years. They are only now altering their approach as the feature article (or human interest story) swamps our daily news. However, if you look at the box next to the pyramid you can see how to incorporate the best aspects of the journalist's trade. The opening sentence and paragraph are the keys to informing the reader. This paragraph contains the most important information. Unlike the essay that starts with a statement of the thesis, the journalist's lead is: who, what, when, where, why and how. In report writing, we want to concentrate on who and what, and then the rest of the 5 W's.

Let's look at how an idea is developed in an essay. The following paragraph represents this approach:

> *Recent research has shown that socialising at work functions can be potentially destructive to collegial relationships and to career progression. While business research has traditionally focused on the benefits of 'networking' for improved work productivity (Jones 2007) and career advancement (Lee 2006), recent research in the fields of organisational psychology and sociology have demonstrated that in the new millennium, the converse may be true.*

The first sentence introduces the main point as part of ongoing research. The second long sentence offers two contrasting ideas: the benefits of networking as opposed to the downside of social activity.

In the following example, the main points are up front in simple declarative sentences with the minor points at the end of each sentence and no reference notes. There are two sentences; in the first one the most important fact comes first, that socialising is bad at work.

> *Socialising at work functions can be harmful to your work relationships and career, according to recent research. Organisational psychology and sociology researchers have demonstrated that in the new millennium networking may not improve work productivity or help career advancement.*

The second sentence has been cut from 44 words down to 22 words. Both approaches work, but the second can be read in one go and the argument is clear. Perhaps it makes the research seem less complex, but it does get the point across.

Here is an example of switching positive information up front and breaking down the facts to two simple sentences. We've also reduced the word count from 26 to 22.

> *Roads and ports assets continue to be adversely impacted by the prevailing economic climate while the infrastructure and communication assets have performed at, or above, expectation.*

> *The infrastructure and communication sector assets performed above expectation. Roads and ports assets continue to be adversely affected by the economic downturn.*

Some of the differences between the essay and report are the use of shorter sentences, less complex constructions, and paragraphs of no more than four sentences.

The ten rules

Let's go over the ten rules we introduced in Chapter 1, then look at some examples of each. Answering the questions they pose will give us the key to effective report writing. From this you will understand the rules that result in clear, easy-to-follow documents every time. Here are the rules again:

1. How many words in a sentence?
2. How many sentences in a paragraph?
3. How do you identify the parts of a sentence?
4. How do you recognise active and passive sentences?
5. How do you use the dependent clause or modifier?
6. How do you recognise an adverb when you see one?
7. How do you know where to use a pronoun?
8. How do you use the semi-colon and colon?
9. How do you know where to put the comma?
10. How do you know when you're finished?

Rule 1

The first rule is the most important, that is, no more than 25 words to a sentence. Think of your sentences as containing one idea — one sentence, one thought. The object here is to give each idea the space necessary for the reader to comprehend it in one go.

Here is an example of a very long and confusing sentence.

As a small business owner who has already acquired a bit over $100,000 in loan debt, I find Smith and Johnson's rejection of the small business tax offset to be short-sighted and insensitive to the experiences of many businessmen who are struggling to compete in the retail market only to face enormous financial burdens at the close of each financial year.

This sentence has 61 words in three parts. It states who the author is; it challenges a statement by Smith and Johnson; and it says why the author disagrees with them. Below, I have broken it down into four separate sentences so that the author's contention is clearly stated.

I am a small-business owner who has acquired over $100,000 in loan debt. Smith and Johnson are wrong in rejecting the small business tax offset. They disregard the experience of businessmen who struggle to compete in the retail market. These

entrepreneurs run into enormous financial burdens
each financial year.

These two examples show how you can use simple sentences to convey several ideas in an easy-to-read format. The original is a single sentence of 61 words. I have written the same information using four sentences totalling 49 words. The longest of the four sentences in the second example is 14 words. My four-sentence version conveys the same ideas as the first example. But they are easy to read and are also more forceful sentences.

In the second example you can easily locate the verbs in the sentences: 'acquired', 'are ... rejecting', 'disregard', 'struggle', 'run into'. The same verbs are almost hidden in the first example. Each of these short sentences carries a forceful idea in a simple format.

Rule 2

Paragraphing is the subject of Rule 2 and it is an important visual element in documents. By limiting the number of sentences in each paragraph to three or four, we allow the reader to digest and evaluate each section. We also provide white space for the eye, which improves readability. The ultimate form of anti-white space is the long, margin-to-margin disclaimer we have to read on websites and either 'accept or disagree'. These statements are not meant to be read. The writer has deliberately avoided paragraphs and white space in order to discourage reading. No paragraphs, no white space, no reading. To write reader-friendly documents, we provide short, clear paragraphs of three or four sentences.

Rule 3

Visual readability is enhanced when we follow Rule 3, the parts of a sentence. In the previous example, each of the four sentences follows the 'subject–verb–object' structure. The original sentence starts with a dependent clause:

> *As a small-business owner who has already acquired*
> *a bit over $100,000 in loan debt …*

We have to wait to get to 'I' to find out what the issue is: that the author refutes a conclusion made by Smith and Johnson.

In our version, the sentence starts with 'I' ('I am a small-business owner ...') and then follows with the description 'who has acquired over $100,000 in loan debt'. Now we know both who is talking and the author's claim of experience to refute a conclusion made by Smith and Johnson.

All the sentences in my version start with the subject and follow with verb and object. They use the simple English sentence construction. It works. You can vary this, but try to keep to the formula. The criticism is that writing subject–verb–object is boring. I don't think so. In report writing, we want the reader to be unaware of the structure and just get the information. Using a passive sentence once or twice will be enough to vary the pattern.

Rule 4

This brings us to Rule 4 about passive and active constructions. Writing manuals have condemned the passive voice. In fact, it seems the passive voice is a slippery slope — the more you write sentences using the passive voice, the more you want to write them. The mark against it is that passive sentences are longer than active ones and the subject can be ambiguous or hidden. The passive sentence might use more words to make its point than an active sentence.

Sam hit the ball. (active)

The ball was hit by Sam. (passive)

or

The President vetoed the budget. (active)

The budget was vetoed by the President. (passive)

In each case, the passive has two more words and the person doing the action is at the end of the sentence. In the first example, the passive is awkward and doesn't work. In the second example, we can choose the passive to stress the budget or use the active to emphasise the President — both work. So the passive voice can be used to vary simple active subject–verb–object sentences to shift the focus. It is also useful when we want to hide the subject or the doer of the action.

Two people in this department made serious mistakes.

Mistakes were made.

The second, passive sentence hides the perpetrators while still admitting to errors. We sometimes need to do this in business in order for the flow of work and communication to continue.

The goal is to try to identify a passive construction when you use it and decide if it's necessary for one of these reasons. Sometimes it isn't easy to do. But when you know if your sentences are active or passive, you've taken control of your writing. When you make a decision to use one or the other of these, you are in full control. That's what we are trying to accomplish — taking control, as if you were the editor of your writing.

Rule 5

We can use our original example to deal with Rule 5, the question of how to treat a dependent or independent clause. (Remember, a dependent clause is a group of words without either a subject or object. It's an incomplete sentence. When it has a subject and object, it becomes an independent clause or complete sentence.

See the previous chapter on grammar.)

> *As a small-business owner who has already*
> *acquired a bit over $100,000 in loan debt, I …*

The sentence starts with a long dependent clause so we have to wait to locate the subject, 'I'. Compare this to the revised example below, which gives the subject in the first word.

> *I am a small-business owner who has acquired over*
> *$100,000 in loan debt.*

We identify the 'I' immediately. The rule here is: always put the dependent clause at the end of the sentence and start the independent or main clause with the subject.

A dependent clause acts as a modifier of the independent clause. By placing the dependent clause at the end instead of the beginning of the sentence, we allow the main subject clause to be forceful and lessen the modifier. Compare these two examples:

> *I like this job because it is interesting work.*

> *Because it is interesting work, I like this job.*

The first example is direct and we know what the subject thinks. In the second example, we have to wait and don't get the stronger effect of the main clause.

There are identifiable marker words that indicate what follows is a dependent clause, such as 'after', 'although', 'as', 'as if', 'because', 'before', 'even if', 'even though', 'if', 'in order to', 'since', 'though', 'unless', 'until', 'whatever', 'when', 'whenever', 'whether', and 'while'. When you use one of these as your opening word, you are writing a dependent clause. That's a signal to change the direction and put this clause at the end of the sentence.

Rule 6

Another modifier is the adverb, covered in Rule 6. It is a word that can modify a verb, an adjective, another adverb, a phrase or a clause. It is a complicated part of speech but we can locate most of them by their ending, that is, 'ly'. This includes words such as 'probably', 'recently', 'appropriately', 'basically', 'briefly', 'angrily', 'rudely', 'carefully', 'surprisingly', 'sadly', 'successfully', 'hurriedly', 'brightly', 'smoothly', 'highly', 'leisurely', 'eagerly', 'patiently', 'rapidly', 'easily', 'unfortunately'. There are many more without 'ly' endings but let's concentrate on these because they are the ones we usually overuse. (If I take out 'usually', the last sentence is stronger.)

These words undercut the verb and alter the meaning. In some cases, this is necessary. You will increase the coherence of your information if you save these 'ly' words for narrative or essay writing and limit them in report writing. By now, you get the point that report writing is meant to be forceful and direct so the information is easily understood.

Rule 7

Rule 7 introduces a useful but problematic word, the pronoun. I have a simple formula for using pronouns: they should be close to the nouns they are representing. I mean close in terms of space. The closer the pronoun to the noun, the easier it is to understand the meaning of a sentence. Compare these examples:

> *The CEO called a meeting. He delivered the positive*
> *sales figures for the week.*

*The CEO called a meeting. The department manager
attended. He delivered the positive sales figures for the
week.*

Distance means confusion in the second example; we don't know if the CEO or department manager delivered the sales figures. This can prove difficult in long involved paragraphs. Keep your pronouns close to their nouns and you will avoid uncertainty.

Also, vary using nouns and pronouns and don't rely on 'it' — the most overused pronoun. An easy editorial exercise is to locate every 'it' and replace most of them with the noun. You will avoid confusion and increase clarity.

Rule 8

Rule 8 deals with the semi-colon and colon. The semi-colon presents a problem since many writers believe using semi-colons raises the intellectual level of their writing. I don't know if this is true, but I do know that using them in report writing brings confusion. Misuse forces the reader to re-read sentences to get their meaning.

As discussed in the previous chapter, the semi-colon is used to join two independent sentences that are closely connected. The writer is indicating to the reader that the ideas in the two sentences are inextricably linked. It is a device that reveals the writer's intention to the reader. This is not appropriate in business writing. Avoid using semi-colons and you will increase readability. Semi-colons don't belong in business reports where the main purpose is communicating facts and information.

Another use of the semi-colon is separating a list of three or more items. This is a simple device and, to avoid confusion, you can use commas instead of semi-colons. So, I've effectively taken the semi-colon away from report writing. You will have a chance to use this punctuation in other formats but not in business writing.

The colon is less problematic. Its usage is easy to understand. A colon introduces a list of bulleted items, such as:

- *Investors can hedge their option by short selling.*

- *Issue will be viewed as debt on the balance sheet.*
- *Investors will not have a stake in the project.*

You can often combine a list within a sentence and use a colon to introduce it, such as:

You can use the following punctuation: a comma and conjunction for compound sentences; a semi-colon for three or more items in a list; and a full stop (period) to end.

Don't overuse colons.

Rule 9

I have already covered punctuation in detail in the previous chapter, but one of the most used marks is dealt with in Rule 9, concerning the comma. However, because we rely on simple, direct sentences in report writing, the comma is used infrequently. That is because it is better to use a full stop, rather than a comma, in writing reports. There are times when the comma conveys precise meaning about who is performing the action and it can't be omitted:

The employer said the employee was lazy.

The employer, said the employee, was lazy.

In the second sentence, the comma tells us it is the employee who is speaking and that it is the employer who is lazy. It is important to know when to use the comma with good effect.

Rule 10

When do you know that you have finished? The simple answer to Rule 10 is when you have to submit it. This means you work as an editor right up to the last minute, thinking of ways to increase clarity and understanding for your reader. After all, you are writing for the reader. I predict that once you get the bug for editing and simplifying your report writing, you won't be able to stop. Someone will have to ask you, 'Is that report ready?' That is when you re-state your recommendation or conclusion and then stop.

Résumés and cover letters

One final writing task, and probably the most important, is the job résumé or CV. If you go into the world of business as an employee or employer, you will encounter this document. You may have to read dozens of them in your capacity as manager. Or you will have to keep your own résumé up to date as you progress in business. The résumé will be with you throughout your career. In a sense it's your calling card. Now, let's find out the essentials of a good résumé.

If you know your reader, you are able to write a cover letter that focuses on the job being advertised. This will require some careful pre-writing (see Chapter 1, 'Technique') or research about the company. The cover letter should be brief and to the point. Those in charge of reading it might have to go through many résumés. He or she will give yours a few seconds before moving on. Here is where you can apply the business box. You need to search for that opening sentence that somehow makes you shine among a group of similar cover letters. That's putting the most important piece of information first. What can it be?

You might have to pore over the company website if they have one. Maybe you will visit the actual offices sometime before the application deadline. If the job means enough to you then you will find the clue.

Once you get the reader's attention you will try to answer all the criteria they have set out. Remember, at this point your goal is to get an interview, not necessarily the job. That comes during the interview. You will concentrate on summarising your experiences that fit the job being advertised.

The letter focuses on the reader and the résumé gives a broader picture of you. It is a history of your job experience but not a long-winded one. Again, keep in mind that the reader will only look at the résumé if the letter prompts him or her to do so. How long should your résumé be? In Australia, résumés of two pages are acceptable but no more than that. In the United States, résumés of one page are the norm. In the United Kingdom a one-page résumé is called a CV (curriculum vitae). But in the United States, a CV is a long, detailed explanation of the applicant's education and research career. It is used only by academics. Follow the format for the country where you are seeking a job. If you have connections in the industry, try your CV or résumé out on a friend. The population of job seekers is bigger in the United States and the United Kingdom. The competition may be greater but you still have to grab the reader's attention to get that interview.

In all your report writing you will benefit from outlining if the task runs a page or more. You can do this informally. Follow the business box model (p. 58) and put the most important information in the first paragraph. Whether it is your covering job letter or an analysis of investment opportunities, you should provide the crucial information up front. Your reader could even stop after that paragraph. You might want to include a key background fact as well.

For example, if you had to write a report on whether your local city airport should be renovated and enlarged to accommodate increased passenger traffic, your outline might include:

Recommendation: best option for increasing airport capacity

- *council committee option (recommended)*
- *non-council and other options (not recommended)*

Background: key pros and cons for taking up this option

- *positive outcomes*
- *negative outcomes*

Restatement: Council committee option will fulfil necessary requirements.

(If this were an essay outline it would look very different. See Chapter 5.)

The paragraphs follow the business box outline with information given in decreasing importance. When you have a paragraph for each of the salient facts you need to get to your reader, you can summarise them in the final paragraphs. This could mean a restatement of the conclusion as in your opening paragraph. When you do several outlines, you will find this a useful way of starting that report that's due next week.

4

NARRATIVE WRITING

Tell the story

The simplest approach to narrative writing is to tell a story. Everyone loves a good story. Now we have to know what we are talking about with stories. You can make everything up, which is called fiction. That is, you can write a novel or a poem. We are writing non-fiction but we have the same ingredients as in fiction — people and events. Only in our case it all has to be true, using actual people and real events, and we must present these elements in an ordered form that resembles a plot.

What kinds of non-fiction narratives are there? Well, biographies and autobiographies, memoirs and profiles, travel articles, feature stories from magazines and family histories. These are all real life stories about other people or yourself. So the basic structure of a narrative involves character, setting and plot. You must shape these elements to make them interesting to your reader.

When we write a narrative, we are telling a story that features people rather than sources and facts, and communicates experience through the five senses. We want to give a sense of the individuals, of the place, of the time and, most important, a sense of drama. The narrative has a beginning that grabs a reader's attention; a middle that keeps the reader engaged; and an ending that lingers in the reader's mind like the reverberations of a gong.

Voice

Before you start your project, you must make an important decision. What voice will I use to tell the story? We call this first person, second person and third person. Let me explain. When you tell a story using the first-person format, you speak directly to the reader who knows only what you reveal. It is an intimate form of address and we sometimes call this, the 'I' voice. Here is an often quoted example of voice by Steven Figg from his article, 'Understanding Narrative':

> *I am sitting on top of the cold sandstone wall, gazing at the horizon. I am worried that I might fall off and hurt myself.*

The disadvantage of this is that we can only see what the narrator tells us. We don't know if he will fall or not.

The next voice is called second person, which is not used often for narrative writing but I have used it in this book and it is a common address for many non-fiction writers. It's the 'you' voice as in:

You see him sitting there on that wall. You wonder what he's thinking about. You imagine that he may fall.

Second person is an easy, colloquial style and allows the writer to talk directly to the reader. It works well in how-to and cooking books that adopt a narrative style.

The most widely used non-fiction address is third person. Here the writer knows everything about the events and characters and can even attempt to pry inside their minds. The writer can relate to the reader what the characters might be thinking and feeling:

Humpty Dumpty is sitting calmly on top of the sandstone wall, gazing at the horizon. He wonders whether he might fall off and hurt himself.

Writing from a third-person position gives the writer full control of the setting, characters and events. It's a powerful way of getting to your reader. Choose your voice and then begin.

Telling your story

So where do you start when you are trying to tell a story? The first, almost too obvious, answer is at the beginning — *no!* There might be some stories that should start at the beginning, but nine times out of ten your reader will stop before you have got far. If we consider that the most important ingredient of a narrative is people, then start with them.

The easiest way to do this is to get a quote from one of your important characters and use it to open your story. The quote should suggest what will happen in the rest of the story and pique the interest of your readers. They should say to themselves, 'I wonder why they said that?' Here's what I mean:

I was born in the house my father built.

This is the very promising opening line of President Richard Nixon's autobiography. He was a controversial person and this seemingly quiet but evocative sentence sets a new tone for the reader. The following examples are more direct:

After losing three multi-million-dollar businesses,
I finally found the formula for success.

People call cooking an art, and I have ten steps that
will make you an artist.

See how it works? In each case the quote leads the reader to want to know more and this is your main thrust in the opening sentences. Unlike the report and essay, the narrative needs to keep the reader anticipating the next set of events as your story unfolds.

Let's look at each of the main points separately.

Characters

Character covers the people you are going to write about. It's helpful to make an outline of the traits of your people, that is, draw a picture of them with words, such as:

Sophia was at least 6 feet tall. Her skin was black-
gold and her eyelashes curled over her eyes. She
wore a faded T-shirt that was too small for her.

In these three sentences, we were able to include at least five descriptive traits.

You must draw on actual experience with these people. Sometimes you will know them only through other writers. They may not be alive or available. You will have to find accurate depictions of them to fit into the story. Here's where the fiction writer has an advantage. They can make it up, but you can't. You are bound to be true to the real life people you are writing about. An advantage over the fiction writer, however, is that you know the events and ending before you start and you probably already understand their significance.

Events

Now that you know who the people are, you need to tell the reader the key events in their lives. You should do this, otherwise the reader will say, 'Why should I care about them?' This is called the 'grab', that is, the significant dramatic event that makes your subjects interesting to the reader. What will grab them? For example:

My first encounter with the CEO of Hawkins Aviation was watching as he crash-landed his Cessna. He crawled from the smoking wreckage and said, 'Where do you want to have lunch?'

The grab is something like the first few minutes of a television drama. Usually, the program gives a sequence with characters in action that makes you want to continue viewing. In non-fiction narrative, you have to make the reader see the people as you do — as fascinating, unpredictable, accomplished and prone to difficulties and problems. These are the human elements that make all of us want to know more about people who accomplish great or significant goals. You are their chronicler, explaining their actions and interpersonal relationships.

Shaping your story

When relating the dramatic events of your characters' lives, you have a difficult but interesting task. You may know what happens to each of the characters but the question is how to present these events to readers so they are both intrigued by and enlightened about the subjects. This is called the 'shape' of the story. This is a non-fiction version of the 'plot'. For example, you can use a series of events that unfold chronologically, that is, day by day or year by year. But to dramatise these events, you might have to jump from one to another. Look at these examples and decide which one more closely fits your purpose.

> *It was a cold wintry day in Portsmouth in 1862 when the Luscombe family, eight children and two adults, prepared for their journey to Australia.*

> *John Luscombe remembered the cold wintry night when his family, eight children and two adults, set sail from Portsmouth to Australia.*

Which one of these makes the reader want to continue? Is it the testimony of one of the characters or a description of the day? Making such decisions is your task and you need to have a lot of information about your characters in order to have choices and to be able to shape these events into a sense of order. This will work, for example, for a profile of someone you think is important or for the family history that you are preparing to distribute to relatives. Who are these people and how do they relate to me, they will ask.

Progressing your story

You are doing the work that will make reading enjoyable and insightful. You have sorted out your characters, amassed the events in their lives and started with a provocative opening. Many writers get stuck into the research and have pages of detail and photographs to match. Whether it is a biography, a family history or a travel article, the next step seems too difficult. Readers want to know: Now what?

This is called the opening-sentence syndrome, which was covered in detail in Chapter 1. The solution is to have a set of starter sentences when you are ready to write. Try them out. Here are opening sentences for a family history.

Our family name appears in the 11th century Domesday Book. We were wealthy at that time and

I am going to find out what happened to us in the next 1000 years.

This opening works well, not just in writing the first sentence of the narrative, but in starting the whole writing process. That is, by writing the first sentence you are able to finish the paragraph, the chapter and even the book. You might like your first sentence or change it later. Either way you have started. Keep going.

Paragraphs and chapters

The thread of the narrative has to come alive. To do this you can follow a few simple techniques. The first has to do with the building blocks of narrative structure — paragraphs and chapters. Think of paragraphs as the bricks that go into building chapters. In fiction, such as a novel, you can invent dialogue between characters. However, with non-fiction this is difficult. Unless you can substantiate an exchange of dialogue through research or directly from the subject, you have to be careful about truth and accuracy. So most paragraphs will consist of description and paraphrasing.

Paragraphs advance the action of the characters. Keep paragraphs short, that is, no more than four to five sentences. Look for a hook or a kind of insight at the end if possible. Most of the time, you won't be able to find one but when you do it will help to keep the action moving, such as: 'We traced the family name from England to America in the late 19th century. Then, it disappears.' That is the end of the paragraph. We can start the next paragraph with, 'I located it again in 1920 not far from our last address.'

As with paragraphs, keep chapters short, that is, no more than eight or ten pages. Like the paragraph, you must find a hook at the close of each chapter. It is essential that the reader has a reason to continue reading. Here's an example:

> *After six months at sea, the Luscombe family had changed irrevocably. A new and unexpected leader had taken over. But not everyone was accepting of this change in status.*

The key here is not to spend too much time on the first draft looking for the hook at the close of each chapter. You want to keep the flow of the story going but, at the same time, make an editorial note to return to that section for a final edit revision (covered in Chapter 1). You can always improve your writing and ability to shape each page. Learning how to allocate time is part of training to be an editor of your own writing.

The sentence

We have gone through the paragraph and chapter structure of a narrative. There is another crucial element in becoming a good storyteller — the sentence. Understanding how to incorporate drama into sentences when necessary will give you greater control over your writing.

We discussed how paragraphs and chapters are like building blocks. The same construct can be used for a sentence. Think of sentences as individual bricks, where you decide what each brick delivers to the reader. You can arrange them in a fitting order. You decide the order because you are in control of the writing.

> *He opened the box, fumbling with the flaps, until he reached inside and felt the warm, tingling sensation of a living animal.*

He touched the warm, tingling animal inside the open box as he fumbled with the flaps.

In these two sentences, we have the same information presented in a different order. Which one is more dramatic or suits the narrative's purpose? Revisit Chapter 1 for more on sentence structure.

Setting

Let's now go over another important aspect of the narrative — the setting. Where do the characters live and how does their environment affect their lives? You need to decide how important this is to telling the story. For example, it might be the key to the entire story as in:

When the Luscombe family left for Australia from Britain in 1862, they were approaching an unknown continent and landscape that would alter the family's fortunes for the next 150 years.

Or it might simply be something in the background that adds a bit of colour to the overall events in the life of your characters. Here is the foreboding setting as foreground from the opening lines of Truman Capote's non-fiction book *In Cold Blood*:

> *The village of Holcomb stands on the high wheat plains*
> *of western Kansas, a lonesome area that other Kansans*
> *call 'out there'.*

Most of what we have discussed so far has an underlying theme. Everything you write must be controlled by you. Take a strong hand and look at each sentence for clarity. Ask yourself if it does what you intend in the manner that you want the reader to understand.

Applying the ten rules

Now that you have the basic elements of the narrative, you can apply the ten rules to writing it. For Rule 1, the length of the sentences, we know that short declarative sentences will work best. Keep the length to 25 words but allow quotations to run longer for accuracy. People rarely speak in grammatical language. They hesitate, use complicated verbs and sometimes leave out the subject. You, as the writer, provide the necessary grammar, always indicating any omissions with ellipses (the three full stops that indicate where words have been omitted) and using parentheses to indicate any material you have supplied to aid comprehension.

We have discussed Rule 2, paragraphing, in terms of content and allowed at least five sentences to a paragraph. This rule can be broken if you are building towards a climax in a paragraph, but don't stretch it too much. In other words, there are no ten-sentence paragraphs.

You can also break one other rule in paragraphing. With report and essay writing, we steer clear of one-sentence paragraphs but not in narrative writing. Here it depends on what a single sentence is meant to accomplish, for example:

> *There was a shout of 'Fire!' and everyone sprinted to the exits.*

One sentence here is enough to make the point. Using quotes always means shorter, easy-to-read paragraphs.

Rule 3, covering parts of speech, remains the same: subject–verb–object. In narrative writing, keep the action moving forward and without hesitation. In storytelling, sometimes a breathless avalanche of events keeps the reader enthralled. That means relying on Rule 4, using active sentences where the 'doer' is the subject and action is the result. Characters move the story forward so make them the subject as often as you can. They seem to take over the story and you must keep up with them:

> *He made his presence known to every one of his relatives whether they liked it or not.*

The passive sentence tends to stop the action and can be used as a kind of brake. It's as if you are travelling fast and then need to come to a full stop, as in:

> *The final decision to advance or withdraw must be made today by the Generals, not the Prime Minister.*

Again, knowing when and how to use these sentence structures means you are in control of the writing.

With Rule 5, regarding independent and dependent clauses, we come to a new way of using these modifiers. (Remember, a clause is a group of words with a subject and verb. If it also has an object, it is a complete sentence.) Unlike report writing, in narrative writing we have to gauge the use of delay and modification in allowing our story to progress.

The use of a dependent clause at the opening of a sentence could mean delaying the crucial sense words for maximum anticipation. With a report, we don't strive for drama, but in a narrative we are always searching for a sense of excitement. So, in a narrative, put the dependent clause up front, delaying the information in the independent clause until the sentence is finished. For example:

> *When he finally opened the door, he came face to face with a skeleton.*

The same approach applies to Rule 6 concerning adverbs as modifiers. We don't avoid 'ly' words but, as in the essay, we don't overuse these tricky, adjusting words. You can assert ideas and motivations as 'probably', 'invariably' or even 'rarely'.

Rule 7 concerns pronouns, which can present a problem to the narrative writer. You will use a lot of them and you need to be careful how they are placed. The same explanation as in report writing applies — keep them close to the noun they represent and don't rely on 'it' to carry the meaning. Search for 'it' in your document and keep them to a minimum. But for 'he', 'she', 'they' and 'his', 'her', 'them' and others, you will determine if there are too many or too few pronouns. Here is a case where the writer has too many pronouns:

> *He taught our team that if you don't work hard and apply yourself, you can't be the best that you can be.*

As opposed to this rewritten version:

> *The coach said that hard work and application would make us a better team.*

The first sentence has five pronouns. In the rewrite the sentence ends with one. It still gives the same meaning but is crisper and to the point.

Using semi-colons and colons is less restrictive in narrative writing. Rule 8 for narratives explains that the semi-colon is a useful tool, particularly when you have two events that come close together. However, this punctuation mark should be used sparingly. The same is true for colons in narrative writing. Both are useful but not often needed. Rely on the straightforward English sentence and keep the action moving.

Punctuation marks are inserted in all forms of writing, so you will use them in reports, essays and narratives. However, applying Rule 9 to narrative differs from its use in other structures. Narratives use quotes and paraphrasing which always requires some form of punctuation. You will need to use the comma to control the meaning of the sentence. Consider this example:

> *Patrick said the carpenter is a poor worker and a bludger.*

> *Patrick, said the carpenter, is a poor worker and a bludger.*

The comma guides your reader to understand the change in voice and be clear about who is speaking. In the first case Patrick is speaking and in the second the carpenter has his say.

For narratives, you want to concentrate on pulling readers into your story. They need to enter into your world, and elaborate stylistic devices are not very helpful. You must rely on your words.

Unlike other forms of non-fiction writing, the narrative dictates its own ending. Usually, there are events, deaths, court cases, goodbyes and hellos that mean the end. That's when you apply Rule 10 and stop writing. Your story is over.

5

ESSAY WRITING

Think it through

We write essays to change people's minds, to make them think. The essay is an exploration. The standard format is: introduction, body and conclusion. Here's what a formal essay outline looks like:

Title

I. Introduction

  a. Premise/thesis

  b. Background points

II. Body

  a. Point 1:

    1. Supporting information

    2. Supporting information

  b. Point 2:

    1. Supporting information

    2. Supporting information

III. Conclusion/summary

  a. Summary of supporting information

  b. Conclusion reached and why

(Restatement of premise)

You don't have to coordinate your thoughts so thoroughly but it helps in thinking through your argument. We learned this format in school and many of us have been practising it for years. The structure is easy to follow. We write about a subject because we see a problem, want to discuss an issue, or decide to analyse an event.

Here are two examples of essay thesis subjects based on car manufacturing and agriculture.

> *Was the government support for the car manufacturing industry justified and did it succeed?*

> *Should the government allow foreign ownership of our agricultural industries?*

In each case the opening sentence starts with a premise or proposition. This may remind you of the classroom when your teacher put the premise or problem on the screen or board and analysed it for you.

Let's look at the three sections that make up the essay — introduction, body and conclusion.

Introduction, body and conclusion

The **introduction** involves stating the premise of the essay and taking a point of view for the reader. You will need a sentence giving the background. You might add that the government has been pouring in millions of dollars in loans to keep the car companies going. You'll then consider if this is positive or negative. You might add that each of the major car companies has paid back their government loans.

You've started the reader thinking about the proposition and now you have to find a transition to filling out the picture. This is the **body** of the essay. It means putting the background material into focus for the reader. You will have done research and gained knowledge about the proposal. Let the reader take that journey with you. Show how you understood the background and where you got your information.

The crucial issue here is linking, that is, the ability to link together sentences, ideas and paragraphs. This is the journey and the reader will want to follow you down that path if you make it interesting. Consider stylistic items such as pace, content and expansion. Use these elements to bring the reader along. Not too fast or they won't follow. Not too slow because they will get ahead of you. It is a test of your ability to make sentences and paragraphs understandable, informative and worth the journey.

Before you reached this point you probably had to decide what your purpose is. Is it to present a full, truthful and fair analysis of your subject? Or are you more intent on showing the strength of one position versus the other variables? Essays can be written to promote a point of view that the writer feels strongly about. They can also move over to propaganda, which is the weighting of sources to tell only one side of an argument. How you arrange and discuss your background sources will lead the reader to travel with you or to reject the road you are clearing.

Here are two ways of looking at the same proposition:

Illegal immigration is a major problem for the government.

Migrant workers who cross the border pose a problem for the government.

Which one are you more interested in? Which one will the reader follow? Telling readers what they want to hear can be seen as pandering to dominant opinions. Telling them what they don't want to hear means they might not read your essay. The body of the essay gives the reader as full a picture as the length of the essay can afford. Ideally, it should lead to the final part — the conclusion.

The **conclusion** is the point where all the research and analysis come together in the essay. By now readers have grasped your point of view, understood how it is related to the background and research and, if you have been skilful and adept, they will read the conclusions as their own thoughts. That's the best result, but there are other reactions that are acceptable. You might have come to conclusions that the reader acknowledges but doesn't agree with; or your conclusions, though plausible, go against ingrained feelings or beliefs. In all these cases, you have persuaded the reader to follow your thoughts, accept your trail of research and stay with you until the close of the essay. That is success.

Approaching your essay

Now let's find out how to achieve this goal. There is a method for writing a straightforward essay and there are tools to help you reach the reader. The rules explained in writing narratives and reports also apply to the essay: writing short sentences, keeping the pronoun close to the noun, avoiding repeated words or phrases and using full stops instead of commas.

However, there are a few differences when writing an essay. The main departure is how you link sentences and paragraphs. With the narrative, quotes and action take precedence. You link these elements through suspense and drama, that is, you try to keep the reader engaged in wanting to turn the page or read the next paragraph. In a report, facts and information are the essentials. Every paragraph should contain a significant piece of information and readers can stop at any point when they feel they have enough information to react or respond.

In the essay, linkage between sentences and paragraphs is based on *your* thoughts. You must weave a thread that connects one thought to another and doesn't allow the reader to stop or stray. With every one of your thoughts the reader is carried forward. Here are some key strategies that help to connect your sentences and paragraphs.

- Short term to long term: e.g. 'Will government subsidies secure a future for the automobile industry?'

- Most important facts to least important: e.g. 'The Normandy invasion began on 6 June 1944 and there are many individual stories intertwined in this event.'

- Chronological: e.g. 'Our family name was first recorded in 1892 at Ellis Island.'

- General to specific (deduction): e.g. 'To reduce the accident rate, using mobile phones while driving should be made illegal.'

- Specific to general (induction): e.g. 'The company has defaulted five times on its bank loans and has no cash on hand. It is clear it will declare bankruptcy at the close of the financial year.'

Your goal is to decide on a strategy for developing your idea and then link your sentences and paragraphs in a way that draws the reader to your argument. Here you need linking phrases (the kind I suggested you avoid when writing a report or narrative), such as:

- However, it has …
- On the other hand …
- It is intended now to …
- Following on from …
- Associated with …
- Another cause of …
- Alternatively, a document may …
- Contradictory evidence suggests …
- In the case of …

These connecting phrases link the points in your argument. Unlike the report and narrative, linking is the key to essay writing. It's as if you are constructing a series of highways for the reader to travel down. When the path is clear and the signposts are working, the reader knows where he or she is going.

An effective method for keeping your reader interested is the use of a list. Think of the essay list as a complete sentence broken up for easy reading. There are two kinds of lists you can use in an essay.

- The first is complete sentences for each point (as in this list).
- The second starts with a sentence, with separate points for each item.

With the complete sentence list, we still have to use parallel formatting and keep each sentence relatively the same length.

With the itemised list, you need:

- a series of points
- an introductory sentence
- a closing sentence
- a full stop.

This is one way to set out the full sentence list. It means you have treated each of the points separately with only one punctuation mark at the end — a full stop. We can rewrite this list with full punctuation.

With this list, you need:

- a series of points;
- an introductory sentence;
- a closing sentence; and
- a full stop.

In this list (above), we have added all the necessary punctuation marks of a complete sentence. The only difference is in the way we set it out on the page. It could also be written as follows: 'With this list, you need: a series of points; an introductory sentence; a closing sentence; and a full stop.' Here you avoid the separate list format. So the only reason for setting this as a list is that it will gain meaning or recognition by doing so. You have to make the choice. In essay writing the list must be justified, not as information but as contributing to the meaning of the paragraph.

Applying the ten rules

We can now apply the ten rules to essay writing. Rule 1 takes us into uncharted territory, that is, sentence length. Short sentences are still the aim, but the key is not the number of words but how each sentence works within the paragraph. While we try to keep sentences to a readable length, they may go over the 25-word limit and sometimes by quite a stretch. Can your sentence be read in one go? Is it understandable? You must answer these queries to your satisfaction.

Paragraphing is also different. Rule 2 explains that essay paragraphs must have a beginning, middle and end. They follow the same structure as your essay in miniature. This means they could contain six or seven sentences and sometimes even more. Again, provide the reader with a reason for following your train of thought. You still must take into account the use of white space and avoid long page-length paragraphs.

Because the essay brings in as much internal experience as outside research, it also uses the widest variety of sentence structures to achieve its aims. The writer will vary Rule 3 concerning the use of subject–verb–object, perhaps trying different forms. You can even experiment with Rule 4, using active and passive sentence structures. In essay writing you must be clear but also adept at making your intentions known.

By now, you should be aware that the essay is probably the most complex form of non-fiction writing you will encounter. The conundrum is that it is also the most common form, especially with the advent of the Internet. It is also the form most likely to bore, anger, mystify, confuse and, at the same time, fail in its aims. However, when the writer gets it right, the essay can be a delight, a revelation, a whole new way of looking at any subject. That is why most of the ten rules are different for this form of writing.

A grammatical device useful in essay writing is the dependent clause as in Rule 5. In report writing we tried to limit using dependent clauses and if necessary placed them at the end of the sentence rather than the beginning. With the narrative, we allowed the use of a dependent clause but with the caveat that it would slow down the action. In the essay, we rely

on the dependent clause to work in its most effective way —
as a modifier. Here the clause moderates or explains the major
independent clause:

> *After you have mastered the intricacies of the game,*
> *you will become a competitive player.*

Without the opening clause, the sentence loses its meaning.
For the essay writer, modifying and expanding are how points
are made. You are telling readers you know all the sides of this
point and then guiding them to the main thought and clause.
You keep the key points in the main independent clause but
broaden the reader's view with the modifier.

> *Once you learn the intricacies, your golf game will*
> *improve and you will become a competitive player*
> *over time.*

The essay writer has to become skilled at varying both
complex double-clause sentences and simple ones to create an
end point. Each sentence is like a miniature of the full essay
structure. Here are three sentences of differing length and result.

Scientists agree that if the ozone layer collapses, the global community will suffer and we may not recover. We must act to stop this from happening. This is certain.

Another departure in the essay structure is the use of adverbs, as in Rule 6. We avoided them in report writing, used them sparingly in narratives and now retrieve the adverb and put it to good use. Because modifying and explaining are valued in essay writing, the adverb works perfectly in helping the writer to keep from being dogmatic.

We know it usually rains at this time of year.

He recently took up golf and will probably take lessons if he is serious about the game.

In each case the adverb softens the statement, gives it a human touch and avoids rigidity.

The pronoun, as in Rule 7, is a tricky device in essay writing. It certainly undercuts the formality of an essay. Using 'I', 'me', 'we' or 'us', called personal pronouns, usually means direct intimate language. I have heard that some writers try to keep them out of essays completely. If you try this, you will end up with a very complicated piece of writing. You will probably have to write a passive sentence to avoid using a pronoun, for example:

> *This text is being written using Times New Roman*
> *font.*

rather than:

> *I'm writing this text in Times New Roman font.*

Your decision to use a pronoun must be based on clarity and the need to avoid repeating proper nouns. If you keep the pronoun close to the noun it represents, it will serve you well.

Another important essay device is the semi-colon, as in Rule 8. Yes, I told you to avoid using this punctuation in writing reports and narratives. In those cases, the semi-colon worked against your purpose, undercutting and modifying what should be direct and unequivocal sentences and paragraphs.

However, in the essay the semi-colon is a useful and important device. Deftly using the semi-colon can mean stringing together important and complete sentences that build like a crescendo of information. The semi-colon is like an off-ramp in your highway; it directs readers to make the connections to each element in your reasoning so they don't lose your assembling of facts and argument. For the accomplished essay writer, stringing together sentences through the use of semi-colons can be a powerful device in winning the reader over to your point of view.

> *Many how-to books start with the whole; this one starts with the parts; others start with the materials; all of them are necessary.*

The semi-colon in this case keeps the thought building and working in the reader's mind. If the ideas are captivating then the reader will continue in order to know what the end will bring.

The comma in Rule 9, like the pronoun, presents something of a problem for essay writers. Writers usually can be divided into two groups: those for whom the comma is an essential tool, and those who never use it. There are a lot of us who fall between these two schools of thought. If we are allowed to use more complex forms of sentences in the essay, this means we must also learn how to make the comma work for us.

Lynne Truss, in her book, *Eats, Shoots & Leaves* deals with commas and more from the point of view of clear writing. Her classic example of a sign saying 'No dogs please' shows how a simple comma clarifies meaning. 'No dogs, please' was the intention. You will need to experiment here with your essay writing style to incorporate the comma as a useful device.

Rule 10 dictates how to close your essay. You can now refer back to the original outline for your final paragraphs — the conclusion. Summing up, pulling all the threads together, and making it work will test you at the close of your essay. The conclusion either makes sense after all your statements, facts and arrangements or doesn't. You will know if you have succeeded and you must give this last bit a lot of attention because this is what your readers have been waiting for, what they have stayed with you for and what they expect. It is the payoff.

The descriptive essay

There is a particular type of essay that leans heavily on useful punctuation. I am thinking of the descriptive essay that asks the writer to depict something — an object, person, place, experience, emotion or situation. The idea here is to create a written account of a particular experience or to describe a person who may or may not be known to the reader. The descriptive essay allows for a great deal of artistic freedom. The goal is to provide an image that is vivid and moving in the mind of the reader.

The descriptive essay doesn't follow the usual structure. In fact, with this form you have to get the reader's attention in your opening paragraph. You will need to rely on vivid language and the ability to look for details that will interest a reader. If you are writing a profile, you should concentrate on what your subject has to say, that is, good quotations. You can start your essay with a provocative quote and draw the reader in. If you are describing an event, give the most exciting moment in your opening paragraph. Since you have a limited amount of research, you will have to rely on emotions and feelings as well as the ability to paint a picture with words.

This type of essay is close to the narrative. We mentioned that narrative sometimes finds its way into both report and essay writing. In newspaper feature essays the two forms will often be used together. Everything we learned about narrative can help us in elaborating the essay, though the purposes of the two forms are different. With the descriptive essay, you use a story to expand the point of view in your piece. The description doesn't overwhelm the ideas.

The academic essay

We have looked at general and descriptive essays, which we read in newspaper columns and feature articles and now often on Internet blogs. However, most of us encountered the academic essay sometime during our education — in high school or university. This is a specialised form of essay which is designed for classroom work.

Since the essay demonstrates the writer's ability to link

and build ideas, the reader — in this case teachers or examiners — can almost see into the writer's mind. They can determine if the writer's ideas are sound, well developed and persuasive or the opposite. The academic essay is a perfect tool to help evaluate a student's skill as writer and thinker. It is distinct from the research paper, with its reliance on evidence and footnoting.

The essay develops ideas and concepts through the writer's thought process and should be both concise and clear in purpose. You know from the statement of the thesis in the first paragraph what the essay will discuss. Since academic essays usually appear as exam questions, it's important to write the thesis sentence according to the guidelines and instructions. Sometimes it helps just to repeat the question, such as:

Should the bill banning mobile phone use while driving be passed?

followed by your essay answer:

Research shows using a mobile phone while driving is a cause of serious accidents. This essay will make the case for why a bill banning use of mobile phones while driving should be passed.

You will follow the same introduction–body-conclusion framework as for a general essay, but you need to concentrate particularly on logical transitions between these three sections. The reader must know when you are making your jump from one to another. There is a formula for writing the expository essay — the five-paragraph structure.

In this format, the writer has an opening paragraph determining the exposition, three paragraphs providing background and research, and a concluding paragraph summing up the findings and choosing sides. In all, five paragraphs encompass the essay. It is a simple but effective way to approach a straightforward essay-writing task. You can start with a clear, concise thesis statement in the first paragraph in three or four sentences. Stress addressing the question asked, not going off on tangents:

Australia has embraced multiculturalism as a policy. Issues of intercultural communication have become more prominent in the workplace. However, little has been written on this subject, and many organisational managers have no training or knowledge of how to deal with people of diverse cultures.

Follow with your evidence, the facts you have gathered to make your case. You have three paragraphs to build your research into a forceful case. Once you have accomplished your task, you can draw your conclusions. This is not just a restatement of the thesis but a new and convincing position based on your three paragraphs of evidence.

As a simple approach to the essay, this structure works well for impromptu or spontaneous assignments. You set out the formula and follow the five-step approach. The expository format can also work for argumentative essays. Here, you are taking sides in your writing rather than simply discussing an issue.

Academic and argumentative essays are similar, but the argumentative essay differs in the amount of pre-writing research involved. The argumentative essay is commonly assigned in advanced composition courses and involves a good deal of research. Expository essays involve less research and are shorter in length. They are often used for in-class writing exercises or tests. The main difference between the two forms is that the argumentative essay requires investigative research and a forceful conclusion with the writer clearly taking a point of view.

By now, you realise that the essay is a specialised form of writing and requires a variety of skills. A valuable link to essay writing is the website www.aldaily.com. Here you can choose among a daily offering of essays from English-language journals around the world. Read them to enhance your skills and enlarge your world view.

6

EMAIL WRITING

Plan the message

Email writing involves writing for the small screen. With all the devices available to us, we are reading and writing on a variety of screens, some larger than a page and others much smaller. Right now, one of the most common methods of moving information among readers is the email. We rely on it both for business and personal contact.

There are two kinds of emails: the conversational and the informational. Conversational emails are part of the world of social media. They have become integral to connecting people to people. They are short, repetitive and quickly erased. How do you communicate with your friends, your colleagues, your contacts, your teachers, your students and many others? You might use Facebook, Twitter and email interchangeably. Whatever you choose, for business purposes the email is the information conduit. Learn how to use it concisely and then adapt it when you move on to another medium. Information emails require some research or thinking and organising before they are completed, and they leave a trail so that if we keep the email we can refer to its contents at a later date.

Here are four emails — each a version of the same conversation — that demonstrate how the same information can be presented in differing ways:

Email 1

From: Martha Smith <msmith@yourmail.com>

Subject: Chairs

Date: 15 April 2013 9:30:22 a.m.

To: Susan Goods <sgoods@mymail.com>

1 attachment, 8.7 KB

Hi,

I want to let you know what is happening with the order you gave me on 4 March. You asked me to get 50 ergonomic desk chairs for our new staff offices and to place this order with the Purchasing Department. I contacted Purchasing on 7 March and talked to Henry Cable, the person in charge of buying office equipment for our company. I called Henry again on 20 March to confirm delivery of the chairs. I was told Henry was no longer with the company and no one else knew what had happened to the order for desk chairs. I did some research and found out that the supplier of desk chairs was Atom Office Furniture. On 2 April, I called them and they could not find a record of the order. I believe someone in the company probably had the order so I decided to wait to see if the chairs would arrive on time. I haven't done any follow-up and unfortunately, we have not received the desk chairs.

Martha

Email 2
From: Martha Smith <msmith@yourmail.com>
Subject: Desk chairs
Date: 15 April 2013 9:30:22 a.m.
To: Susan Goods <sgoods@mymail.com>

Hello Susan,

On 4 March you contacted me to order 50 desk chairs. You indicated that we had to have the ergonomic desk chairs by 15 April to satisfy the company's health and safety requirements.

On 7 March I placed an order for the chairs with Henry Cable in purchasing. On 20 March I followed up to confirm delivery of the chairs. I was told that Henry was no longer with the company and no one else had any information.

Since we had a sample of the desk chair, I was able to locate the company that manufactured them. I called them and explained that we had ordered the ergonomic desk chairs. They searched their inventory and orders and had no record of our purchase.

I have contacted the purchasing department in writing and asked for a complete explanation of the situation. However, in consequence, we will not be able to meet the health and safety requirements.

Regards,
Martha

Email 3

From: Martha Smith <msmith@yourmail.com>

Subject: Desk chair purchase

Date: 15 April 2013 9:30:22 a.m.

To: Susan Goods <sgoods@mymail.com>

Dear Susan,

I am writing to let you know that your order of 2 March for 50 ergonomic desk chairs from the purchasing department will not arrive by the April deadline. I have researched this order and offer the following results:

- I ordered the desk chairs on 4 March with a delivery date of 14 April.
- On 10 March, I discussed our order with Henry Cable in purchasing.
- I called purchasing on 20 March to confirm the order and was told there was no record of the order.
- I contacted the Atom Office Furniture company on 14 April and found out they also had no record of the order.

This is the sequence of events so far. Please let me know what my next step should be.

Regards,
Martha

Email 4 (with revised bullet points)
From: Martha Smith <msmith@yourmail.com>
Subject: Desk chair purchase update
Date: 15 April 2013 9:30:22 a.m.
To: Susan Goods <sgoods@mymail.com>

Dear Susan Goods
I am writing to let you know that your order of 2 March for 50 ergonomic desk chairs will not arrive. I have researched this order and offer the following results:

- 4 March received order for desk chairs — delivery date 15 April.
- 10 March discussed and sent order to purchasing.

- 20 March tried to confirm the order and was told there was no record.

I then contacted the Atom Office Furniture company, the supplier, on 14 April and found out they also had no record of the order. This is the sequence of events so far. Please let me know what my next step should be.

Regards,
Martha Smith

Decide which of the four you think communicates best to the intended reader; however it should be clear that the last one is the most concise. Clearly, organising your information in a logical (in this case chronological) order helps the reader to digest the information at the first reading. If we think of the hundreds, even thousands, of emails delivered in a working day to one company, we can see why this matters.

The first email requires deciphering, that is, it must be read several times to find the information and, even then, it is not clear. The second email adds some white space to the page. You can see this instantly; the email is easier to read even though the information is almost the same as that in the first email.

The third email introduces the bullet list, which is a concentrated way to target information. However, the bullets are a bit long and not easy to read. The last email, with cleaned up bullet points, you'll agree, sets out the information visually and concisely. You don't need to re-read or ponder the meaning. In fact, you can make a decision immediately.

An email should run to no more than one page. If you need more space then you are writing an attachment or what is called a short report. There is a technique for this kind of writing that also works for the email. Both short reports and emails strive to impart information in a quick and direct manner. This is particularly important in business where email traffic is constant.

Subject heading

Some business people may get up to one hundred emails a day. They need a method for screening which allows them to open emails that matter. There are spam detectors that help and other devices. Another helpful device is the subject heading.

If the sender has paid attention, that heading tells the reader whether they need to open the email. Everyone who writes business emails should provide a subject heading that tells the story. Look at the headings from emails 1 to 4: 'Chairs', 'Desk chairs', 'Desk chair purchase' and, finally, 'Desk chair purchase update'. The progression adds information that tells the reader what to expect. Do they have to open it? The subject heading should never be more than four words. Think of it as if you are writing a newspaper headline.

Compose your emails

Another tip for writing concise and accurate emails is to look at how you compose them. By this, I mean have a look at the way most of us respond to emails. When you get one it's similar to getting a phone call. You want to answer it quickly and the sender usually expects an answer within a day. The process is familiar: open the email and read it; decide what needs to be answered; type out your response then click on the reply button and off you go. Wrong!

Instead of working with email software, which provides no editorial help, open a file in your Word software and write your email. Whatever IT consultants or computer geeks tell you about email software, it is unusable by committed writers. We need the tracking, grammar and spelling checks of Word as well as the thesaurus to compose an intelligent email. True, some of the software might not transfer but the final email can be reformatted.

Not only does this give you more writing power, you probably have Word open already. One more important advantage to writing first in a Word file is that you have an extra step between the reply button and the send button. You have to copy and paste and then look it over one more time before hitting 'send'. That gives you one last opportunity to make sure it's right.

How many times have you sent an email and then realised you forgot to add something or you didn't check the spelling (always difficult to do in email software)? Or you lacked tact. This is especially useful if you have a full page of information that requires thinking and decisions. Your email recipients will thank you for taking the time. I've heard that 'you will be known by your emails'.

The visual impact of emails

We can learn another helpful tip from the four sample emails beginning on p. 129. The second email was a big improvement on the first because it broke up the long paragraph and provided white space. Paragraphing can help keep your reader's eyes relaxed and able to see without straining. You can test that by trying to read those long, single spaced, margin-to-margin legal notices. They say 'don't read me' very loud and clear. If you are writing to be read, give the reader white space. I average from four to five paragraphs on a page. I try to keep to that use of white space in my emails too.

Good typography in printing tries for the same result. This relates to questions about using a particular typeface and point size, or how big the margins will be for your long report. There is always an optimum arrangement of letters and white space for any document. You don't have to ponder this, just look at your result and ask yourself if it is easy to read. When you copy and paste your Word file to the email, you'll soon see whether the result looks good.

Using bullet lists

Two of the sample emails, the third and fourth, have bullet lists but the last is the best. There are a number of ways to write bullets. If you are clear about who your reader is, you will choose the right format.

There is a method to accomplish an effective set of bullet points. For report writing, a bullet list is an abbreviated way to convey information that will be discussed in detail or is simple enough to digest in a brief sentence. Look at these three versions of a bullet list below.

Example 1
Other items to be noted:
- The Fund issue would be listed on the stock exchange. Reporting requirements to this exchange are expected to be similar.

- Investors can hedge the option by short selling. While this will create some downward pressure on the share price, these investors have a fixed conversion ratio and therefore will be price sensitive when setting their hedge. Short selling is likely to occur prior to conversion also.
- The issue is likely to be viewed as debt on the balance sheet.
- Investors are not likely to be existing investors and therefore they are unlikely to participate in the capital raising.
- The issue will use private placement capacity affecting the amount of stock that can be issued by this method over the following 12 months. There could be a request that the placement capacity be refreshed by current investors.

There are a number of attractive features, which warrant further investigation.

Example 2

Items to be noted:

- Stock exchange reporting is similar on both exchanges.

- Investors can hedge their option by short selling at a fixed price.
- Issue will be viewed as debt on the balance sheet.
- Investors will not have a current stake in the project.
- Amount of stock issued is limited but can be changed at the general meeting.

These features are covered in detail in the report.

Example 3

ITEMS TO BE NOTED:

- **Stock exchange:**
  Reporting requirements are similar on both exchanges.
- **Short selling:**
  Investors can hedge their option by short selling at a fixed price.
- **Balance sheet:**
  Issue will be viewed as debt.

- **Investor profile:**
  Investors will not have a current stake in the project.
- **Private placement:**
  Amount of stock issued is limited but can be changed at the general meeting.

These features are covered in detail in the report.

Example 1 appears as a jumble of words, not very different from the email in our original set of examples. We have to pull the meaning out of it. The reader has to do the work the writer should have done. It also breaks the rule about white space: everything is packed together without separation. You can get a headache trying to read these bullets.

The second example does a better job. We have simplified the items and indicated that they will be discussed in detail later in the report. A bullet list shouldn't try to give all the information — it is an abbreviation, not the full explanation.

With bullets, the reader looks down the page first. So the first two words in the list are the most important. That's why I have bolded those two words for each bullet point in example 3. Your eye is drawn to them. Whether you use example 2 or 3, you still read down the page. These two starting words must be parallel (the same part of speech) and packed with meaning. Don't start with throwaway words such as 'the', 'an', 'however', etc. Here we are using the format for report writing — getting information out. For more on writing effective lists, turn to p. 112 in Chapter 5, 'Essay writing'.

One more item to note is the question of parallel format, that is, each phrase begins with the same part of speech. It is a form of balance and rhythm to help deliver your meaning. Here are two examples:

> *My degree, my work background and ability to take on new projects qualify me for the job.*

> *My degree, my work background and my ability to take on new projects qualify me for the job.*

The first sentence breaks the parallel format and the second, by adding 'my' in the last phrase, adheres to it. This is a handy method to use especially when writing bullets. Let's look at another example:

- Prepared construction plans.
- Purchasing new equipment.
- Changed the building orders.
- Will contact construction engineers.

These bullets are difficult to read because they express confusing timelines. Here is the same list with parallel formatting:

- Preparing construction plans.
- Purchasing new equipment.
- Changing building orders.
- Contacting construction engineers.

The word at the start of each bullet point is a gerund (i.e. it ends in 'ing'). These words give the list an active progressive style. The reader can also scan down the page and get all the items in a single view. Keeping your lists and bullets parallel will help you to reach the reader quickly.

Lists, white space, parallel formatting — these are the tools that allow you to write concise, short and understandable prose for your emails. All of these techniques can be used on any kind of equipment. Remember, it's not the hardware that determines what you write nor is it the software. They are there to make the task and turnover easier. The real work is still putting the words together, which we once did with a pen and paper. The language has evolved even when the mechanics have leaped forward. We need to practise to become both better writers and more connected to our intended readers.

GUIDE TO USAGE

The following guide provides tips on understanding the differences between similar yet different words, an overview of grammar and a guide to standard spellings and usage.

Similar but different

ability, capacity: Ability is being able to do something; capacity is the potential to do it.

about, approximately: About is inexact; approximately implies accuracy:

We are about halfway there.

It takes approximately 1 litre.

accept, except: Accept is to receive willingly; except means to exclude.

adapt, adopt, adept: When you adapt something, you change it to suit a purpose, such as adapting a novel in order to make a movie. When you adopt something you take it as is and make it your own. Adept means highly skilled, an expert: 'She is adept at her work as a seamstress.'

adverse, averse: Adverse means opposite; averse means reluctant.

advise, advice, inform: Advise, a verb, means to offer suggestions; advice is a noun, as in 'Take my advice'; inform is to communicate information.

affect, effect: Affect means to influence; effect as a verb means to bring about, and as a noun means result.

a lot: A lot is a colloquial, vague expression meaning very much or very many; avoid using the phrase 'a lot' in writing. Alot is a misspelling of a lot.

all ready, already: All ready means to be prepared and already means previously.

all right, alright: All right meaning safe, is correct: 'His performance was all right.' Alright is an incorrect spelling.

all together, altogether: All together means in unison; altogether means completely.

among, between: In general, use between for two items or people and among for more than two items or people.

amount, number: Amount refers to a bulk or mass: 'No amount of money would be enough.' Number refers to individual, countable items: 'He took a large number of stamps.'

appraise; apprise: Appraise means to judge and apprise is to inform.

as to: This is an indefinite way of saying 'about', 'of' or 'whatever'. Avoid it.

because of, due to: Because of means on account of, while due to denotes attributed to.

beside, besides: Beside means next to and besides means in addition to.

Capitol, capital: The Capitol is a government building and capital is financial assets or the city where government is located. London is the capital of England.

censor, censure: To censor something is to edit, remove or prohibit it because it is judged objectionable. To censure someone is to strongly condemn him or her as wrong.

cite, site: Cite means to quote and site is location.

compose, comprise: Both refer to the relationship between a whole and its parts. Compose refers to the bringing together of the parts that make up the whole. Comprise refers to the whole that includes its parts.

continual, continuous: Something that is continual is repeated often. Something that is continuous goes on without interruption.

convince, persuade: Convince means to make someone believe something; persuade means to get someone to do something.

different from, different than: When comparing two things, use different from: 'The movie is different from the book.' If 'different' introduces a subordinate clause, use the conjunction 'than': 'The true story was different than I had believed.'

disinterested, uninterested, bored, boring: Disinterested means impartial or having no opinion; uninterested means you don't care; and bored is lacking interest in something; boring refers to something that induces boredom.

divided into, composed of: Something can be 'divided into' parts and it can be 'composed of' parts. They are not interchangeable.

e.g., i.e.: The abbreviation e.g. (Latin: *exempli gratia*) means 'for example'. Do not confuse it with the abbreviation i.e. (Latin: *id est*) which means 'that is to say'.

etc: Abbreviation for etcetera and means 'other things of the same kind'.

every one, everyone: Every one means each one of a group of particular people. Everyone means all, everybody.

farther, further: Use farther to refer to distance and further to denote degree, as in 'further research is necessary'.

fewer, less: Use fewer for individual, countable items or people; use less for (non-countable) bulk or quantity: 'We expected fewer people to come. They stole less than $20.'

finalise: Use 'complete' instead or a simple word.

firstly, secondly: The 'ly' is unnecessary; use first or second, or use the numeral.

hopefully: It means full of hope, not probably or maybe. Avoid it.

impact: Can be wrongly used as a verb. Wrong: 'Will that impact on the office?' Right: 'What impact will that have on the office?'

implicit, tacit, explicit: Implicit means implied or unstated; however it can also mean without reservation. Tacit means unspoken, not expressed openly but understood and is similar to the meaning of implicit. Tacit is sometimes used in reference to speech: 'His speech gave her the tacit approval she needed.' Explicit is the opposite of implicit, meaning clearly and openly stated.

imply, infer: Imply means to suggest something indirectly. Infer means to conclude from facts or indication.

influence, affluence: Influence means to have an impact on, while affluence refers to riches and wellbeing.

irregardless: Not a word, use regardless.

its, it's: Its is the possessive of it: 'The tree lost its leaves.' It's is a contraction meaning 'it is': 'It's too bad we can't come.'

libel, slander: Legally, slander means to defame someone orally in a speech or public remark. Libel is to defame someone by any other means such as in print, pictures or films.

passed, past: Passed is a verb: 'I passed the test.' Past is either a noun, an adjective or a preposition but never a verb: 'The past haunts us.' Or 'We have just walked past my old school.'

practise, practice: Practise is used as a verb to mean doing something to improve your skill. 'I practise the piano every morning.' Practice as a noun means doing something regularly and refers to the act itself: 'You need more practice.' In the US only, practice is used as both the noun and verb.

precede, proceed: Precede means to go before in time: 'His remark preceded the program.' Proceed means to move forward: 'Before we proceed, we should be sure of the rules.' Don't use proceed as a fancy word for 'go'.

preventive, preventative: Preventive and preventative mean the same thing but choose preventive.

principal, principle: Principal as a noun means the head of a school or a sum of money; principal can also be used as an adjective meaning the first or foremost. Principle refers to a fundamental or guiding truth or belief.

rebut, refute: When you rebut an opponent's argument, you speak or write against it. When you refute an argument, you disprove it.

shall, will: Shall has generally been replaced by will in modern usage. Shall is sometimes used to indicate a commanding tone: 'You shall eat everything on your plate.'

that, which: That, without a comma, is used for a restrictive clause (a clause essential to the meaning of the sentence); which, with a comma, is used for a non-restrictive clause (one not necessary to the meaning of the sentence).

then, than: Don't use then (which means at that time) in comparisons. Use than: 'He is wiser than (not then) his father was then.'

unique: No other adjectives are necessary (e.g. *most* unique) since it means one of a kind.

usage, use, utilise: Usage means established practice. Don't use it as a substitute for the noun 'use'. A more common tendency is to replace the verb 'to use' with utilise and the noun 'use' with utilisation, but this is not recommended.

who, whom: Who is a substitute for 'he', 'she', 'they'; whom substitutes for 'him', 'her', 'them'.

whose, who's: Whose is the possessive of who. Who's is a contraction of who is. 'Who's going to tell me whose jacket this is?'

Grammar

Adjective: A word that modifies a noun.

Adverb: A word that modifies a verb, an adjective or another adverb.

Agreement: The verb must agree with its noun e.g. 'The cat walks into the garden. Cats walk into the garden.'

Ampersand: The symbol for the word 'and': &. Use it when it is part of the official name of an organisation.

Apostrophe: Use it to show possession: 'This is Brian's car.' Use it to form contractions: 'don't'; 'can't'.

Asterix: *Use it to refer to a footnote.

Clause: A group of related words but, unlike a phrase, a clause has a subject and a verb.

Cliché: A trite or overused word or expression — avoid them.

Colon: Use primarily when introducing a list, a quotation or a formal statement.

Comma: The most frequently used internal punctuation in sentences.

Comma splice: When two independent clauses are joined by a comma instead of a full stop e.g. 'He's always late for meetings, it makes me angry.' Avoid.

Complex sentence: Contains one independent clause and one dependent clause.

Compound sentence: Has two or more independent clauses, joined by conjunctions and no dependent clause.

Compound subject: Refers to more than one subject in a sentence.

Conjunction: Words that join or link elements such as 'and', 'but'.

Dash: A punctuation device. An **em dash** is a dash the width of the letter 'm'. Used in the same way as brackets or commas in a sentence. An **en dash** is a dash the width of the letter 'n'.

Used to replace the word 'to' (e.g. 'the show will last 2–3 hours').

Ellipsis marks: Use three spaced full stops with one space before and after to indicate the omission of words from a quotation e.g. 'Ask not what your country can do for you ... do for yourself.'

Future tense: A verb tense indicating the action will occur in the future using helping words such as will or shall. 'He *will leave* at noon tomorrow.' 'We *shall overcome.*'

Gerund: A noun created from the 'ing' form of a verb e.g. 'She went swimming yesterday.'

Jargon: The specialised language of a field or profession.

Modifier: Describes or limits another word or group of words.

Noun: a word that names a person, place or thing.

Paragraph: Develops one idea with a series of logically connected sentences.

Parallel construction: To be clear, a sentence must be consistent. Avoid shifts in person, number, verb tense or voice.

Paraphrase: Involves borrowing someone's idea that you rephrase in your own words.

Parentheses, brackets: Use ( ) or { } to set off non-essential expressions.

Parts of speech: There are eight parts of speech: noun;verb; pronoun; adjective; adverb; preposition; conjunction; interjection.

Past tense: A verb tense indicating an action is finished or completed: 'She *went* to the dentist on Tuesday.'

Phrase: A group of related words that cannot stand alone as a sentence and has no verb.

Preposition: A word that shows a relationship of one word in the sentence to another word in a sentence, such as 'about', 'between', 'by', 'down', 'during', 'for', 'in', 'to', 'over', 'into'.

Present tense: A verb tense that indicates the action is occurring now: 'The geese *are flying* overhead', 'He *sees* the ball and *raises* his bat.'

Pronoun: A word that stands in for a noun.

Punctuation: Helps a reader make sense of what you write; includes full stops, question marks, exclamation points, commas, semi-colons, colons, dashes, parentheses and brackets.

Run-on sentence or comma splice: An error in which two independent clauses are joined without proper punctuation (a full stop/period or a semi-colon).

Sentence fragment: A group of words that is missing a subject or does not express a complete thought.

Simple sentence: Has one independent clause and no subordinate clauses.

Split infinitive: Breaking up an infinitive phrase with one or more adverbs: 'to quickly take'.

Subject: Part of the sentence that tells what or whom it is about.

Subordinate clause: Also called a dependent clause. A group of words that contains a subject and verb but cannot stand alone. It needs to be connected to an independent clause, such as: 'When the book is published (subordinate clause), the author will receive a final payment (independent clause).'

Tense: Refers to the time in which the action of the verb takes place — future, past or present.

Verb: Conveys the action performed by the subject.

Voice: Indicates the form of the verb, whether the subject performs the action (active voice) or receives the action (passive voice).

Numbers, symbols

Use words for one to nine and numerals for 10, 11, 12 …

Don't begin a sentence with a numeral; spell it out instead

Use commas for numbers greater than 9999 (i.e. 10,000 onwards)

Use $10 million

Use per cent not percent

Use % in tables, charts, but not in text

For Australian dollars use AU$100; for US dollars use US$100; for pounds sterling use £100

Date style: 30 October 2014, not the 30th of October 2014; for US: October 30, 2014

Typography

Body text: The continuously read type on the page.

Display text: Headlines, headings and subheadings.

Font: Typeface.

Hyphen: The shortest dash, which we use both to connect words and, at the ends of justified lines, to break words.

Justification: Even text alignment at both left and right margins.

Leading: Line spacing.

Point: The size of the type or text (72 points = 1 inch, 28 points = 1 cm).

Ranged left: Even type alignment at the left margin (also called ragged right).

Ranged right: Even type alignment at the right margin (also called ragged left).

Sans serif, serif: A serif typeface has lines crossing the free ends of its letter forms, while sans serif typefaces don't.

Typeface: Type of a particular design.

Clichés: words and phrases to avoid

acid test

at the end of the day

basically

beyond the shadow of a doubt

bottom line

brainstorm

bury the hatchet

by and large

by the same token

dealing with

dialogue — don't use it as a verb

dos and don'ts

expertise

feedback

few and far between, first and foremost

going forward

grind to a halt

hands on

heretofore

iconic

impact

implement

in regard to

in the final analysis

interface with

last but not least

needless to say

point in time

plethora

state of the art

thus

utilise

vitally important

Use a single word for wordy expressions:

Instead of this:	Use this:
a plethora of	many
the great majority of	most
actual experience	experience
advance plan	plan
advocate for	advocate
as a general rule	as a rule
at all times	always
close proximity	near
edit out	edit
first priority	priority
one and the same	the same
refer back to	refer to
small in size	small
whether or not	whether
in compliance with your request	at your request
inasmuch as	since
perform an analysis of	analyse

first of all	first
the colour red	red
true facts	facts
basic fundamentals	fundamentals
join together	join
at all times	always
until such time as	until
due to the fact that	because
in the event that	if
in the final analysis	finally
in order to	to
by means of	by
for the reason that	because
new innovation	new
separate out	separate

ACKNOWLEDGEMENTS

This book began in my head over 10 years ago. Mark Ramsey started me off on the quest by asking me to solve his company's writing problems. Judith Curr of Simon & Schuster suggested that I put it all in a book and Lizzy Walton of Allen & Unwin directed me to possible publishers. Gareth St John Thomas pushed me to write the book for Exisle that could reach the widest audience. I was fortunate to have an excellent publisher in Anouska Jones and editor in Karen Gee. They knew how to organise the chapters so it all made sense. I've been having a decades long conversation with my wife, Jean Gelman, on all these subjects. She has been my long-term editor and guide.

INDEX

Also by Exisle Publishing…

The Right Word

Making sense of the words that confuse

ELIZABETH MORRISON

The quality of your written English is your passport to both academic and career success. Whether you're a native speaker or learning English as a second language, it's very easy to get confused and make mistakes. This book is your essential guide to mastering the subtleties and becoming an expert communicator.

Divided into three sections, *The Right Word* first examines homophones, those tricky words that sound the same but are spelled differently. Entries are organised alphabetically, with meanings and examples (including colloquial ones) being given to facilitate correct use.

The book then looks at words that often confuse — childish vs. childlike, incredible vs. incredulous, for example — before providing a list of the most commonly misspelled words.

Keep this book by your desk as a ready reference providing instant access to superb English!

ISBN 978 1 921966 04 0